SHAMBHALA DRAGON EDITIONS

The dragon is an age-old symbol of the highest spiritual essence, embodying wisdom, strength, and the divine power of transformation. In this spirit, Shambhala Dragon Editions offers a treasury of readings in the sacred knowledge of Asia. In presenting the works of authors both ancient and modern, we seek to make these teachings accessible to lovers of wisdom everywhere.

Zen
and the
Art of Insight

Selected and translated by

THOMAS CLEARY

SHAMBHALA

Boston & London

1999

Shambhala Publications, Inc.
Horticultural Hall
300 Massachusetts Avenue
Boston, MA 02115
www.shambhala.com

9 8 7 6 5 4 3 2 1

FIRST EDITION

Printed in the United States of America

⊚ This edition is printed on acid-free paper that meets
the American National Standards Institute Z39.48 Standard.

Distributed in the United States by Random House, Inc.,
and in Canada by Random House of Canada Ltd

Library of Congress Cataloging-in-Publication Data

Tripiṭaka. Sūtrapiṭaka. Prajñāpāramitā. English. Selections.
Zen and the art of insight/selected and translated by Thomas Cleary.
      p.   cm.
      ISBN 1-57062-516-6 (pbk.)
      I. Cleary, Thomas F., 1949–   . II. Title.
      BQ1882.E5C55   1999   99-34711
      294.3'85—dc21   CIP

Contents

Introduction

"How do you know?"

What does this mean . . . to you? Does it mean "How do *you* know?"
or "How do you *know*?" Or does it mean "*How* do you know?"

Ordinarily this is just a rhetorical question, used as a retort. The
implications, however, are deeper than customary cliché. One of the
great Taoist Zen masters wrote, "Ordinary expressions and common
sayings accord with the path of sages; you should turn to them for
careful research." From this point of view, "How do you know?" opens
the door to a world of wonderment. Are there reliable sources of
knowledge? Of what can we be sure? How can we know this? Does
mentality materially affect matters of knowledge? Is there a way from
opinion to knowledge? What kinds of knowledge are available to us?
How does what we think we know influence our everyday lives?

If we take the time to ask ourselves "How do you know?"—as a
retort, as a question, as a challenge—we may get at the pivot of our
relationships with our own thoughts and feelings, with our fellow
human beings, and with the world at large. Taken for what it can yield
in these roles, the question contains within it a challenge to the root
of all ignorance and complacency.

The question of how we know what we know and how we know
we know it can be one of the most threatening that can be posed,
because it forces us to examine our most basic assumptions about our-

selves, our world, and our being in the world. Yet it can also prove one of the most intriguing and important questions, for it is a first step into the wider reality beyond the pale of hidden bias and unconscious assumption.

How do we know if our perceptions and beliefs are valid? If we use our own knowledge to check our own knowledge, how can we know we are not revolving in circles? If we use others' knowledge to check our knowledge, whose knowledge do we use, how do we know it is knowledge, and how can we know if or how others know when we ourselves do not know if we know what we know?

If we pursue these thoughts too far, we can quickly paralyze ourselves and lose our sense of meaning; yet if we do not ask ourselves these questions, we cannot know what we may be missing, or misconstruing, on account of unconscious assumptions.

One of the difficulties of approaching within our Western context this issue of how we know is that we have learned to disarm the question existentially by giving it terms like *epistemology* and pursuing it intellectually.

That habit is not peculiar to the West, as Eastern writings show, and it is not an insurmountable barrier to experiential insight as long as there lingers no subconscious assumption that the familiar conceptual or intellectual approach is the only way of understanding or knowing things.

When we view religion in terms of belief and worship, the issue of knowledge is not in question. In dogmatic religion, knowledge is identified with the dogma, and the question of its validity cannot arise without creating a sense of violation or threat to the religion.

To avoid the question, the dogma may be called divine revelation or sacred tradition, but it might be that any rationalization for nonexamination of beliefs will tend to satisfy the unconscious desire to remain at the level of belief and worship.

While this may comfort the bewildered within certain limits, the desire for this comfort may also be exploited to manipulate people, even so far as to turn them against one another in the name of their beliefs and actually divert them from their own best interests in the name of salvation.

For us in the West, who have been exposed to some of the worst religious persecutions in the history of the world, and even today hear of violence for and against religion all around the globe, it may be emotionally and intellectually difficult even to conceive of religion that is not based on dogma, belief, or worship. Yet that is precisely what we find within Buddhism, which aims for direct perception of truth and reality, not defense of doctrine or destruction of dissenters.

There is no doubt that Buddhist teachings have, like other religions, employed various edifices of faith and precept from time to time for the protection and maturation of spiritually immature individuals and communities. It is also beyond doubt that such edifices have been diverted, at various stages of their history, to purposes other than those for which they were originally devised. This is historically true of all institutionalized religions, including Buddhism, as is recorded in the writings of their own sages.

The Buddhist teachings on perfection of insight show, to those who have reached a certain level of maturity and for whom the time is right, how to break out of the shell of cultivated belief and spread the wings of independent vision in the sky of freedom. These teachings lead the way from self-projection's bewildering hall of mirrors into the broad daylight of penetrating insight's open, unobstructed space.

When individuals are still at a stage where they need externally imposed structures of belief and practice to modify unruly instincts, habits, and vices, the nondogmatic, nonsectarian gnostic insight of Buddhism is imperceptible and effectively unavailable. This is also true of individuals who are attached to edifices of doctrine and precept at the level of imposing them on others for power or marketing them for profit. According to Buddhist teachings on this subject, in either case it can be harmful for such people even to hear of perfect insight, so their seemingly ungraspable subtlety is actually a form of mercy to the world.

This is one of the apparent paradoxes of the teachings on perfect insight; they are declared to be for the benefit of the whole world, yet at the same time they are not for everyone. The effect is likened to a powerful medicine that may cure illness but can also damage a weak constitution. Insight can be a shattering experience, beyond the capacity of an immature or unbalanced mind to bear with equanimity.

The Buddhist teachings on insight, furthermore, are of such a nature that certain types of mentality are prone to misconstrue them in harmful ways. Bigots of all kinds, moreover, instinctively fear the insight teachings and deliberately misrepresent them to anyone who will listen. History tells us that the first two grand masters of Zen in China, for example, were actually assassinated by formalists fearing Zen insight teaching would undermine their authority.

Classical Buddhist scripture itself includes the appropriate warnings with its prescriptions, just like modern medicine. Scripture also provides remedial teachings and practices for those as yet unable to benefit from exercises in penetrating insight, as well as advanced material for those who are able to awaken this insight.

There is no one word to fully match the Buddhist term for perfect insight in the English language. In canonical Buddhist Sanskrit the word *prajnaparamita* is used. This term cannot be translated in one or two words, and so it needs expansion on its elements to be understood on the level of ordinary reason and common sense.

The root *jna* stands for knowledge, cognate with the *gno* of the Greek/English word *gnosis* and the *kno* of the English word *knowledge*. This is a very general category of mental function in Sanskrit, however, which is itself subject to further definition by means of prefixes.

The common Sanskrit prefix *pra* is in some senses actually cognate with the still similarly shaped *pre* and *pro* in English (meaning "fore" and "forward"), but its spectrum of meaning in Sanskrit is broader. When used with nouns, the prefix *pra* may convey the senses of "power," "intensity," "source," "completeness," "perfection," "separation," "excellence," "purity," and "cessation."

While the exact meaning of any multimeaning prefix may vary according to the verb to which it is prefixed, when this multimeaning prefix *pra* is linked to the root verb of knowing, in the Buddhist context of the relativity of knower, knowing, and known, then all of these meanings of the prefix are included in the term *prajna* for perfect insight.

For this reason, the complex picture built up by the root *jna* and prefix *pra* cannot be captured by a simple word or term, be it *insight, wisdom,* or *perfect knowledge.* Nevertheless, when actual examples are translated in context, the effect of usage is to enrich the meanings of whatever words or terms of the host language are employed as expedient approximations. Thus words like *insight, wisdom,* and *knowledge* come to have special meanings when used in the context of Buddhist relativism and transcendentalism.

Buddhist insight literature in particular warns readers not to take terms too literally according to their conventional concepts. This is one reason that a lot of Buddhist writing is highly metaphorical.

Some of the richness of meaning in *prajna* can be appreciated by considering it in light of those various senses of *pra* as they relate to scriptural descriptions of what perfect insight is and can do:

It is said that perfect insight is *powerful knowledge* in that it can overcome all delusion and all confusion, while nothing can overcome it.

Perfect insight is *intense knowledge* in that it can penetrate external appearances to intuit the inner essence of things.

Perfect insight is the *source knowledge* in that it is the source of enlightenment, and it is the source of enlightenment because it is insight into the source of everything.

Perfect insight is *complete knowledge* in that there is nothing it does not comprehend by intuitive penetration.

Perfect insight is *separate knowledge* in that it is detached from, and other than, thoughts and imaginations, and yet it is able to separate things in the sense of distinguishing them.

Perfect insight is *excellent knowledge* in that it is more objective than conceptualization, more realistic than mentally constructed versions of reality.

Perfect insight is *pure knowledge* because it is unaffected by inner states or external objects.

Perfect insight is *cessation,* or *terminal knowledge,* in that it emerges through cessation of all views and because its awakening terminates compulsive mental habits and false ideas.

The Buddhist scriptures that specialize in the teachings on perfect insight generally follow a pattern of reasoning to show the intrinsic limitations of discursive thought. This is an exercise in attention, not conceptualization, intended to effect a shift of attention from the conceptual to the intuitive mode. Intuitive insight cannot be directly described, so the shift from linear logic to direct perception is approached by deconstruction of conceptualizations. Hence the term *paramita*, or *perfect*, which literally means "gone beyond."

This method is sometimes misunderstood to rationalize irrationality or dissociation, which are not effective means of awakening insight. Then again, it is sometimes construed in terms of conceptual logic per se and not practiced by those who cannot see its connection to pragmatic penetrating insight.

Irrationalism, dissociation, and nihilism have already been diagnosed in Buddhist scriptures and the commentaries and treatises of the ancient masters, and warnings about them are repeated generation after generation. This is particularly prominent in Zen lore, which is intimately associated with specialization in perfection of insight. Shaku Soen, one of the most distinguished Zen masters of modern Japan, wrote in 1898:

> Nowadays it often happens that those who mistake the "silent illumination" of "realization in the dark" for Zen understanding tend to hate writings as if they were poisonous serpents, and fear the scriptures, treatises, and records of sayings as if they were ferocious beasts, saying that the "special transmission outside of doctrine does not insist on writings." Ah, is that not narrow and low? An ancient illuminate said, "If what is beyond doctrine is clear, then how can what is in the teachings inhibit that? If what is beyond doctrine does not admit the teachings, then what is beyond doctrine is not true either. Why? If a mirror is perfectly clear, it does not choose among images of things. If the images are not reflected, that means the mirror is not clear yet. You are rejecting the images of things on account of the dust and dirt that covers the mirror. If you are on the Great Way, you do not fabricate such views." These can be called words of wisdom.[1]

The exercises in the scriptural teachings on perfect insight are intended for so-called *bodhisattvas*, meaning people essentially devoted to

1. From the preface to *Tenkei Zenji Teisho Hekiganroku Kogi*. Tokyo: Koyukan, 1898, 1908, 1910.

bodhi, or enlightenment; especially the *mahasattvas*, mature people. This does not refer to religious devotion or chronological age per se but to mentality and spirituality. The "silent illumination" of "realization in the dark" mentioned by the Zen master refers to a counterfeit insight that is really a form of self-delusion sought by escapists, nihilists, and others traditionally referred to as immature or weak-minded and unable to profit from teachings on perfection of insight.

These scriptures address their teachings to both men and women in lay life, without any further discrimination in respect to gender or social standing. It is, nevertheless, true that in Zen and Tantric Buddhist traditions insight is personified as a goddess; and in Zen and Zen-Taoist lore on transcendent insight it has been written that it is normally somewhat easier for women to access intuition than it is for men.

Some attribute this to the specific effects of different ways in which men and women have been trained; some attribute it to certain differences in habits of attention and perception resulting from biological differences between men and women. However it may be explained, this is one reason that Tantric Buddhism pictures the model of enlightenment as a man and a woman embracing.

This book contains exercises in perfection of insight from scriptures and treatises specializing in this dimension of Buddhism. These are translated from canonical sources and explained with particular reference to the mystical communion of Zen and pan-Buddhism, centered on perfection of insight beyond dogma and dependency.

Zen
and the
Art of Insight

Scripture on Perfect Insight
Awakening to Essence

❦

1.

If bodhisattvas can realistically comprehend the basis of equality of darkness and light in all matter, when they understand this all things are thus. These bodhisattvas quickly realize supreme perfect enlightenment.

This is also true of sensation, cognition, conditionings, and consciousness. If bodhisattvas can realistically comprehend the basis of equality of darkness and light in all consciousnesses, when they understand this all things are thus. These bodhisattvas quickly realize supreme perfect enlightenment.

The equality of darkness and light
In all things is thus;
Knowing the basis and understanding it,
One attains enlightenment.

COMMENTARY

The equality of darkness and light means the identity of emptiness and existence. In an absolute sense, the essence of things is ungraspable, inaccessible to perception or conception; this is called darkness. In the conventional sense, the characteristics of things can be distinguished, relative to the mental faculty; this is called light. When the "equality of darkness and light in all things" is realized, that means that the ungraspability of things in their absolute essence does not interfere with the discernment of things in their everyday actuality; and likewise everyday awareness of the characteristics of things does not interfere with intuitive insight into their absolute ungraspability. This is the principle of the center, the mean, or the middle way, the Buddhist path of balance based on transcending the world while in its very midst, neither insisting nor denying, neither grasping nor rejecting, neither obsessing nor ignoring. This balance is sensed, practiced, and realized in the context of the totality of life, so the scripture speaks of realizing the equality of darkness and light in all things.

2.

Matter, sensation, cognition, conditionings, and consciousness occur in three natures—a nonexistent nature, a temporary conditional nature, and a true nature. If wise people realize this as it really is, then they do not create attachments to consciousness and do not manifest arousal; their minds are open and clear. Because they no longer develop grasping attachments to consciousness and their minds are open and clear, they can then attain emancipation through the teachings of the Great Vehicle.

COMMENTARY

Matter (or form), sensation, cognition (including perception and conception), conditionings (patterns of activity), and consciousness are the so-called five clusters, a term for a classical Buddhist method of analyzing a human being to illustrate the fact that what we think of as our self or our person is not the unity we imagine it to be. This formula is used repeatedly in this literature, particularly as a starting point for enumerating the elements of all experience, both mundane and spiritual.

The three natures in which the five clusters occur—nonexistent, temporary, and true—must be understood to make sense of the teachings on emptiness and perfect insight that say all things are nonexistent or unreal. The nonexistent nature is also called the purely conceptual nature, referring to the contents of our mental descriptions of things. Those mental descriptions are not the things in themselves, not objective realities as such, and so they are referred to as the nonexistent nature of things. Because our confusions and delusions stem from mistaking subjective conceptualizations or imaginations for objective realities, the teaching of perfect insight says that those "things" we imagine are empty; that is, they are empty of absolute reality. In that sense, things as we conceive of them are called unreal or nonexistent.

That does not mean nothing is there, only that it is not as we conceive it; the teaching says there is another nature, a temporary nature, which is the interdependent occurrence of phenomena. We perceive and describe it as thus and so, but that is our interpretation, not the occurrence in itself. The real nature of things is the essence of their dependent nature without the projected overlay of the nonexistent conceptualized nature.

This distinction of three natures helps the mind to sense and maintain balance between "darkness and light," between detachment and involvement. It is key to understanding, in a practical sense, the seemingly contradictory scriptural statements about things in terms of existence or nonexistence, reality or unreality, purity or impurity, and so on. If this scriptural practice of pseudoparadox were meant to be an exercise in scholastic philosophy, the level of meaning would invariably be defined. The first step of the exercise is to perceive which of the three natures scripture refers to, and in what sense, when it says, for example, that things are unreal or nonexistent. This elementary exercise in discernment is then developed into the capacity to focus attention deliberately on each nature, first individually and then collectively, in order to acquire the mental capacity to combine buoyant freedom or nonattachment with wakeful, conscious participation in the world.

3.

If bodhisattvas develop attachments to forms as they are described and act on them in practice, practicing in this way is acting on the notion of the existence of a real body and also acting on craving for existence. Then again, if they carry out any quest apart from existence, this means they do not really know form.

The same is true of sensation, cognition, conditionings, and consciousness. If bodhisattvas develop attachments to consciousnesses as they are described and act on them in practice, practicing in this way is acting on the view of the existence of a real body and also practicing craving for existence. If, on the other hand, they carry out any quest divorced from existence, this is not really knowing consciousness.

COMMENTARY

Practice based on sensation, cognition, conditionings, and consciousness as they are described may be interpreted to mean meditation on technical definitions of these factors of being rather than on direct experience of their operation. There are, however, also specific symptoms or manifestations of attempts to cultivate spirituality with underlying attachments or fixations on illusory conceptions of what is being cultivated.

Practicing on the basis of attachment to forms as they are described may be readily observed in cults where there is an obsessive attention placed on ritual paraphernalia, regalia, costumery, and mummery, or where rites and practices are defined and hallowed in terms of formalities of sanctified value in themselves rather than prescribed to particular people for specific purposes.

———————

Practice based on attachment to sensations as described can be observed in cults obsessed with unusual sense experiences, cultivated by meditation, prayer, or other practices, which are identified as holy or spiritual by dint of their unfamiliarity.

———————

Practice based on cognitions as described can be observed in both cultic and academic dogmatics, where temporary provisional verbal and conceptual formulations are rigidified into fixed doctrines and rules.

———————

Practice based on conditionings as described can be observed in attempts to carry out religious practices based on egotistical or selfish motives, trying to reach for spirituality in ways influenced by unconscious or unexamined instinctual and ingrained patterns of habit.

———————

Practice based on consciousness as described can be observed in cults devoted to alteration of consciousness as an end in itself. Their futility is in their obsession with changes whose possible value or detriment is unknown to them because they are fixated on identifying their subjective feelings with descriptions of changes believed to be significant or spiritual.

———————

A saying from the famous *Pure Name Scripture* helps to keep these principles in mind: "If you practice the teaching through seeing and hearing, sense and recognition, then that is seeing and hearing, sensing and recognizing—it is not practicing the teaching."

————————

The alternative to this is not a "quest divorced from existence," which may refer to some form of alienated mysticism, or to nihilism, neither of which solves the fundamental problem of obsessiveness. Alienation and nihilism are also forms of exaggeration.

4.

If bodhisattvas do not develop attachments to forms as they are described and do not apply them in practice, they are not acting on the notion of a real body and not acting on craving for existence; and yet they do not carry out any quest apart from existence. This is really knowing form.

Sensation, cognition, conditionings, and consciousness are also like this. If bodhisattvas do not develop attachments to consciousnesses as they are described and do not apply them in practice, they are not acting on the notion of a real body and not acting on craving for existence either; and yet they do not carry out any quest apart from existence either. This is really knowing consciousness.

COMMENTARY

An essential purpose of perfect insight practice, one classically emphasized by Zen teachers, is getting over the stage of dogmatic, fixated relationships with the teaching as it is expressed, understood, applied, and realized. This restores the original flexibility of the teaching as it relates to the needs of the individual at each successive stage of spiritual refinement. Without this flexibility, dogmatized and rigidified versions of the teaching become obstacles to progress, even prisons of the spirit.

Zen master Zhenjing said, "Some people do not trust the buddha in themselves and only rely on a little bit of the reflections and echoes of the ancients as imitation wisdom, as objects of knowledge, as fixed doctrines. They tend to turn away from awakening and get mixed up in sense objects; they keep sticking to them and cannot get free."

Showing the way beyond both spiritual materialism and spiritual alienation or nihilism, Zen master Baizhang said, "Right now, just detach from all things—existence, nonexistence, whatever—and detach even from detachment itself."

The *Scripture on Unlocking the Mysteries* explains, "The characteristic of conceptual grasping can be known through the association of names and characterizations. The characteristic of dependent origination can be known through the conceptual clinging superimposed on dependent existence. The perfect characteristic of reality can be known by not clinging to the conceptions superimposed on dependent existence." *(Buddhist Yoga)* This nonclinging is key to perfect insight, as elaborated below.

5.

Bodhisattvas who are mahasattvas should develop three attitudes toward all material forms. First is an attitude of nonattachment. Second is an attitude of noninvolvement. Third is an attitude of purity of heart.

For this reason, whether the minds of bodhisattvas who are mahasattvas are aroused toward those material forms or not aroused, or greatly aroused or impartially aroused, it all should be realistically and impartially examined. Being able to observe impartially in this way, these bodhisattvas quickly realize supreme perfect enlightenment.

This is also true of sensations, cognitions, conditionings, and consciousnesses. Bodhisattvas who are mahasattvas should develop three attitudes toward consciousness. First is an attitude of nonattachment. Second is an attitude of noninvolvement. Third is an attitude of purity of heart.

For this reason, whether the minds of bodhisattvas who are mahasattvas are aroused toward those consciousnesses or not aroused, or greatly aroused or impartially aroused, it all should be realistically and impartially examined. Being able to observe impartially in this way, these bodhisattvas quickly realize supreme perfect enlightenment.

COMMENTARY

Nonattachment, noninvolvement, and purity of heart are attitudes that open the way to objectivity. Here objectivity is applied to the "realistic and impartial examination" of arousal of mind. Realistic and impartial examination of the arousal of mind helps one to sense tendencies toward subjective distortions in one's relationship with the world.

Zen master Huanglong wrote, "When you do not bring up anything at all, you cannot bear the burden; suddenly realizing you're wrong, your heart is filled with infinite joy. Once poison is gone from your heart, even serpents and tigers are your friends." Not bringing up anything at all means not clinging to things; not bearing the burden of nothing at all means not clinging to nothingness. Infinite joy in the heart is the clarity and buoyancy of the mind unencumbered by obsessions. The friendship of serpents and tigers means the ability to remain unattached, uninvolved, and pure of heart in the midst of all mental activity, even negative thoughts and emotions. This is like the ability of the bodhisattvas to examine realistically and impartially the arousal of their minds even though they are detached.

6.

If bodhisattvas who are mahasattvas see existence or nonexistence in material forms, they do not really know or understand.

The same is true of sensations, cognitions, conditionings, and consciousnesses. If bodhisattvas who are mahasattvas see existence or nonexistence in consciousnesses, they do not really know or understand.

COMMENTARY

To see existence means to be fixated on affirmation; to see nonexistence means to be fixated on denial. To avoid these extremes and maintain central balance, one sees things as neither absolutely existent nor absolutely nonexistent. In a sense, the critical issue is not to see *that* things exist or do not but rather *how* things exist or do not.

Zen master Longji said, "If you affirm the pillar, you do not see the pillar. If you deny the pillar, you do not see the pillar. When affirmation and denial are completely gone, then you gain understanding within affirmation and denial."

Zen master Shoushan used to hold up a stick and say, "If you call it a stick, you are clinging. If you do not call it a stick, you are ignoring. So what do you call it?"

7.

If bodhisattvas who are mahasattvas arouse the intention to dwell in the realm of equanimity, then when their minds seek liberation from material form their minds are moved by form, shook-up and totally agitated. Because of this, these bodhisattvas find it hard to attain liberation.

The same is true of sensation, cognition, conditioning, and consciousness. If bodhisattvas who are mahasattvas arouse the intention to dwell in the realm of equanimity, when their minds seek liberation from consciousness their minds are moved by consciousness; they are shook-up and become totally agitated. Because of this, these bodhisattvas find it hard to attain liberation.

If bodhisattvas who are mahasattvas intend to dwell in equanimity, when they seek liberation from material form, if their minds are neither attached to form nor disconnected, because of this these bodhisattva-mahasattvas skillfully attain liberation.

The same is true of sensation, cognition, conditioning, and consciousness. If bodhisattva-mahasattvas intend to dwell in equanimity, when they seek liberation from consciousness, if their minds are neither attached to consciousness nor dissociated, because of this these bodhisattvas skillfully attain liberation.

COMMENTARY

When the intention to attain liberation and dwell in equanimity is a reaction to disturbance by instability and change, insofar as reactivity is the basis of the intention, that very reactivity accompanies the pursuit of the intention through any subsequent course of action. The Third Grand Master of Zen said, "If you try to stop movement to return to stillness, stopping makes even more agitation." Thus the fixation of the intent renders the enterprise futile. That is why meditation can produce agitation and even derangement in some people. The remedy is the balance described in the scripture here, being "neither attached nor dissociated." The Third Grand Master of Zen said, "Trying to get rid of existence is obscuring being; trying to follow emptiness is turning away from emptiness."

Essentials of the Great Scripture
on Perfect Insight

1.

Insight is provisionally said to be of two kinds; yet being beyond subject and object, they are ultimately no different. Why? When bodhisattvas cultivate insight, they mentally seek the nature and characteristics of things; be it selfhood or selflessness, permanence or impermanence, origination or destruction, existence or emptiness, nothing like this can be found. They do not find any characteristics to grasp and do not conceive any grasping views.

At this time they detach from all views of characteristics and impartially realize the true aspect of all things, which has no duality, no difference, no beginning, no ending, no origination, and no destruction. It is not existent and not void; it transcends all manner of verbal expression and is forever beyond the realm of all mental constructs.

COMMENTARY

When insight is said to be of two kinds, this refers to insightful observation of the characteristics of things and intuitive insight into the nature or essence of things. This passage illustrates the practical combination of these two modes of insight, how one leads to the other. Thorough examination of characteristics leads to realization of their ultimate ungraspability, thus opening up intuitive insight into essence. By virtue of intuitive insight into essence the mind is liberated from fixation on the characteristics of things as conventionally defined, thus enabling observational insight to see ordinarily unperceived aspects of things. This is how the cooperation of these two modes of insight can awaken faculties of creativity and artistry in seemingly mysterious ways. The apparent negativity of the insight formulations—"not this, not that, not the other"—represents the process of clearing the mind of preoccupation with limited views of reality.

2.

Insight is of five kinds: insight into the true aspect of things; observing insight; literary insight; insight into objects, referring to the two truths, absolute and conventional; and auxiliary insight, referring to all beneficial knowledge.

The true aspect of things is the essence of insight. Observing is the characteristic of insight. Literature is the cause of insight. Objects are the sphere of insight. Auxiliaries are accompaniments of insight.

COMMENTARY

It is normal for Buddhist texts to define technical terms differently. In the perspective of Buddhist insight, there is no fixed definition of anything at all and cannot be, because definition is constructed relative to perception. Different definitions have therefore been provided for different individuals and communities at different times, according to their particular stages of development and what they then need to make further progress. Thus the definition of a term, or the meaning of a principle, may in effect change for an individual or a group in the course of progress. Buddhist literature contains many examples of this, including illustrations of what happens when the process either is halted or gets out of hand and produces intellectual dissociation.

In some cases, relatively simple and relatively complex definitions of technical terms may appear in the very same text, as here in this work on perfect insight. A relatively simple definition may be utilized as a way of focusing on basics or essentials, while a relatively complex definition may follow up as a means of outmaneuvering tendencies to oversimplify and dogmatize working formulas. Those who become fixated on any one of the five kinds of insight, for example, will develop corresponding warps and defects of mind.

Fixation on insight into the true nature of things alone destroys the intellect, undermines the will, and fosters nihilism; fixation on observing insight alone results in paralysis through flooding, bias through arbitrary selection, or aimless meandering of mind; fixation on literary insight alone produces sterile intellectualism and imitative poetics; fixation on insight into objects alone splits the mind and divides the attention; fixation on auxiliary insight alone makes one the captive of mundane causes and aims. Zen master Baizhang said that if you seek knowledge and blessings before having realized the absolute truth, you will be ridden by knowledge and blessings and cannot be free to use them freely; if you gain knowledge and blessings after having realized the absolute truth, on the other hand, then it will be possible not only to be free yourself but also to employ knowledge and blessings freely. The important point is that these various aspects or modes of insight must work together in their proper relationships in order to effect the balance and wholeness of enlightenment.

3.

Insight means comprehension because it can comprehend all objects of knowledge.

Insight means no knowledge because if there is anything known you do not know the true aspect.

Insight means destruction in that it destroys the verbal expressibility of all things, whether in terms of nature or of characteristics.

Insight means nondestruction because it witnesses the true aspect without destroying temporal definitions.

Insight means detachment because it is forever detached from all clinging obsession.

Insight means nondissociation because it witnesses the characteristics of all things.

Insight means no detachment or nondetachment because it is not dissociated from anything at all, yet it is detached from everything.

Insight means neither destruction nor nondestruction because it never destroys nor fails to destroy anything.

COMMENTARY

Insight means comprehension first of all because in the absence of comprehension there would be no notion or mention of insight to begin with. The various modes of insight mentioned comprehend the several natures in which phenomena occur—the nonexistent (conceptualized or imagined) nature, the temporary conditional (relative or dependent) nature, and the true (real or perfect) nature.

Insight means no knowledge in respect to the true or real nature of things, defining *knowledge* here as recognition of external appearances. When the mind is focused on recognition of gross external appearances, then insight into the subtlest essence is obscured by preoccupation with the cruder function of ordinary "knowledge." That does not mean, naturally, that ignorance of the evident is itself the way to the ineffable.

Insight is destruction in the sense that it destroys the notion that the essence of things can be captured in words, and it destroys the notion that verbal definitions of the characteristics of things have an exclusive, necessary, and accurate correspondence to the things in themselves. Zen literature abounds in images of smashing, destroying, killing, and so on, all representing the dissolution of rigid habits of thought, including the unconscious habit of confusing descriptions with actualities.

Resolving the problem of confusing descriptions with actualities does not demolish either the descriptions or the actualities. What it does is to place them into relative perspective, so that the mind can operate on the ordinary level without that becoming a form of bondage or a limit to perspective. Description of things, both mentally and verbally, is often useful and necessary to everyday life, but it can become a prison when we forget its origins and its original purposes. When we think what we think is what is, then if problems arise, as they inevitably do in the course of evolution, we tend to try to change things without realizing we need to change our ideas of things. This can result in a sort of involution, which in extreme forms can cause an individual personality, a family, or a social group to collapse inwardly around itself. In the meantime, it creates invisible and unsurmountable barriers to growth and progress. The function of perfect insight is to penetrate this vicious circle and liberate the mind from its closed pattern of disguised self-involvement.

Insight means both detachment and nondissociation because both of these factors are necessary to achieve mental balance. Detachment alone leads to dissociation, whereas immersion alone leads to encapsulation of consciousness. Detachment without dissociation, the middle path of centered balance, is a formula for the coevolution of wisdom and compassion.

Insight goes beyond polarities of detachment and immersion, or destruction and conservation, in that it embodies each and every one of these factors in proper balance, neither too detached nor too immersed, not destroying what is not to be destroyed and not maintaining what is not to be maintained. At first there is pseudopolarity in the process of meditation, concentration, and contemplation; but in the final integration of mental capacities, this provisional polarity is transcended and both the ordinary and the ineffable can be perceived at the same time. This is harmonious integration of the several modes of perfect insight.

Treatise on the
Great Scripture on Perfect Insight

1.

Scripture: By virtue of nonattachment to everything, you should have perfect insight.

COMMENTARY

Again the theme of nonattachment as a quintessential prerequisite to perfect insight is emphasized in scripture. Of course, nonattachment to things does not mean denying or ignoring things. Somewhat more precisely, in the more discriminating language used in the scripture quoted above, this means nonattachment to the nonexistent nature of everything. The nonexistent nature of everything means the way we conceive or imagine things to be, not the way they really are. By nonattachment to conceptualizations or imaginations of the way things are, we can gain access to insight into the way things really are.

TREATISE

QUESTION: What is perfect insight?

ANSWER: Bodhisattvas seek knowledge of all types from their first inspiration; the insight therein recognizing the true aspect of all things is perfect insight.

COMMENTARY

Here it is worth noting the fact that the treatise explicitly says that bodhisattvas, or enlightening beings, seek knowledge of all types from their first inspiration. Knowledge of all types is the omniscience of buddhas, often outlined in terms of ten powers of knowledge: knowledge of what is so and what is not; knowledge of results of actions; knowledge of all sorts of interests of all kinds of people; knowledge of all sorts of realms; knowledge of different faculties, higher and lower; knowledge of all destinations; knowledge of all states of meditation and concentration, including how they are defiled, how they are purified, and how to enter and emerge from them; knowledge of past states of being; knowledge of the conditions in which other beings are to be reconstituted when their present conditions change; knowledge of the end of contamination of mind by anything. These powers of knowledge embrace the five types of insight defined in the treatise excerpted before this one, *Essentials of the Scripture on Perfect Insight*—absolute insight, or insight into the true inner nature of things; observing insight, or direct witness of the characteristics of things; literary insight, or understanding of meanings and expressions; objective insight, or understanding of the absolute and relative realities of things; and auxiliary insight, consisting of "all beneficial knowledge" of whatever kind.

Some of these forms of knowing are part of our everyday experience, based on ordinary necessities. Buddhism teaches that we can enhance these familiar modes of knowledge and also activate others that are not generally familiar but nevertheless are possible, accessible, and of potential benefit to humankind.

For the time being, what is perhaps most essential to keep in mind, based on this teaching, is that the bodhisattva or Buddhist practitioner does not become a devotee of just one form of knowledge, even perfect insight. In the course of time it may be necessary to concentrate on one or another mode of knowing in order to round out the mind of the individual or community, but on the whole it is not enlightening to focus exclusively on a partial capacity. Obsession with the transcendental mode of perfect insight is particularly mentioned in Zen lore, no doubt as a balance to Zen's own intensity in this domain, as a dangerous form of intoxication that can deprive the obsessive individual of common sense. For pragmatic purposes, this important caveat can be brought to mind with relative ease by means of the Zen proverb "If you stare at it, you'll go blind."

QUESTION: If that is so, it should not be called perfect, because it has not reached the limit of knowledge.

ANSWER: The knowledge a buddha realizes is really perfect; the practice of bodhisattvas is also called perfect because it is based on this perfection, referring to the result in the context of cause. In the mind of a buddha, this perfect insight turns into knowledge of all types.

Bodhisattvas cultivating knowledge seek to cross over to the other shore, so it is called perfection. Buddhas have already crossed over to the other shore, so then it is called knowledge of all types.

COMMENTARY

This question addresses the issue of order. As mentioned earlier, too much concern with formal knowledge in the beginning of spiritual studies, beyond what is necessary for ordinary life and for higher orientation, tends to constitute an obstacle or interference. This is one of the meanings of the Buddhist term *barrier of knowledge*, in which consciousness of one mode or level of knowledge itself becomes a barrier to more subtle awareness. Therefore the bodhisattva who is in the process of "crossing over" to the "other shore"—transcending fixation of attention to reach liberation and freedom—needs perfection of insight in order to accomplish this mental transformation. The other forms of knowledge and practice cultivated during this process are employed for the purposes of awakening insight, first by creating a balanced personality and a healthy relationship with the world, then by unraveling the inner knots of thought. Once transcendence has been realized and buddhahood attained, the buddha then "comes back" to the world, equipped with all sorts of knowledge gained in the process, which now can be used for the sake of others.

QUESTION: In buddhas all afflictions and habits have already ended, and their eye of wisdom is pure; they should realistically apprehend the true aspect of all things. The true aspect of all things is perfect insight. Bodhisattvas have not yet ended all contamination, and their eye of wisdom is not yet pure—how can they apprehend the true aspect of all things?

ANSWER: To give a brief explanation, it is like people going into the ocean. Some have just gone in, some have gone all the way to the depths. Although there is a difference between the shallow and the deep, they are both said to have entered. So it is with buddhas and bodhisattvas. Buddhas have thoroughly plumbed the depths, but bodhisattvas have not yet cut off all afflictions and habits, so they have little power and cannot enter deeply.

Suppose someone lit a lamp in a dark room, lighting up the things in the room so that they could all be clearly distinguished. If a bigger and brighter lamp is brought in, making everything even clearer, then you realize that the darkness dispelled by this second lamp was still there with the first lamp. Yet even though there was still darkness with the first lamp, it could nevertheless illuminate things. If there were no darkness left by the first lamp, there would be no light added by the second lamp.

So it is with the knowledge of buddhas and bodhisattvas. Although the knowledge of bodhisattvas is combined with afflictions and habits, it can still apprehend the real aspect of things, just as the first lamp can still illuminate things. The knowledge of buddhas also apprehends the real aspect of things, but without any more affliction or habit, just as the second lamp is brighter and clearer.

COMMENTARY

The *Flower Ornament Scripture* says, "The mind, intellect, and conscious-ness of Buddha are ungraspable. One can know the mind of Buddha only in terms of the infinity of knowledge. Just as space is the resting place of all things, while space itself has no resting place, so also is the knowledge of Buddha the resting place of all mundane and transcen-dental knowledge, while the knowledge of Buddha has no resting place." ("Manifestation of Buddha")

QUESTION: What is the real aspect of things?

ANSWER: Everyone talks about the real aspect of things as if his opinion were fact. The real aspect of all this is indestructible, permanent, changeless, and has no creator. As Buddha says to Subhuti in the scripture, "If bodhisattvas view everything as neither permanent nor impermanent, neither painful nor plea-surable, neither itself nor not itself, neither existent nor nonex-istent, and yet do not entertain these as views, they are called bodhisattvas' practice of perfect insight." This means relin-quishing all views, stopping all talk, detaching from all mental patterns; it is originally unproduced and imperishable, like nir-vana. Such is the character of all things. This is called the real aspect of all things.

COMMENTARY

The key phrase or "eye" of this passage is the first: "Everyone talks about the real aspect of things as if his opinion were fact." The practice of relinquishing views, stopping mental talk, and detaching from men-tal patterns is an exercise employed to gain the objectivity whereby opinion is distinguished from fact. Zen master Foyan said, "If you would like to be free from subjective seeking, just do not conceive opinions and views." As in the writings on perfect insight, the Zen master goes on to make it clear that this practice of detachment does not mean dissociation: "This nonseeking does not mean blanking out and ignoring everything. In everyday life, twenty-four hours a day, when there is unclarity in the immediate situation, it is generally because the opinionated mind is grasping and rejecting." *(Instant Zen)*

TREATISE

As it says in the verses praising perfect insight,
Perfect insight is truly objective, not distorted:
Thought, imagination, and envisioning gone,
Manners of verbal expression also vanish.

COMMENTARY

The ordinary perceptions and notions of things on which we act are conditioned by thought, imagination, mental pictures, and mental talk. All of these inner activities that influence our perception and behavior are also conditioned by other factors, both inherited and acquired. Therefore a temporary cessation of the stream of conditioned thought, imagination, envisioning, and description is employed to give the mind room to perceive things more directly. Terms such as *gone* and *vanished* refer to this practice of halting or stopping the flow of habit; they do not mean to suggest that insightful people can no longer think, imagine, envision, or speak. What cessation means is that the mind is not imprisoned by manners of thought, imagination, envisioning, or speech.

Infinite sins removed,
Pure clean mind always unified—
Such a fine respectable person
Is able to see insight.

COMMENTARY

Buddhist teaching generally views sin as a result of ignorance, in that harmful and evil actions result from misperceptions of realities. These misperceptions may include all sorts of interpersonal misunderstandings, paranoid elaboration of negative emotions, miscalculation of effects of actions, and misunderstanding of self-interest. Cultivation of the ability to stop the automatic flow of compulsive habit energies is proposed to enable the individual to overcome wayward tendencies at the unconscious level. In this way "infinite sins" are "removed."

The "pure clean mind" in Buddhist terms does not mean thinking pure clean thoughts or thinking of good things; it means the mind in its pristine clarity and fluidity, not imprisoned by automatic habits of thought and emotion, aware of everything without being fixated on anything.

> Like space, without defilement,
> Not a fantastic theory, not literal—
> If you can see this way,
> This is seeing Buddha.

COMMENTARY

The *Flower Ornament Scripture* says, "If you want to know the realm of buddhahood, make your mind clear as space." This formula is used in classical Zen to represent the path of central balance in which there is neither attachment nor dissociation. Space contains everything, yet nothing adheres to it; similarly, the mirrorlike mind sees everything without fixation on anything. This is not a fantastic theory, nor is it meant literally, in the sense that it does not propose that the mind be literally empty or blank. It is likened to the clarity of a mirror, in which everything is then reflected impartially.

> If you truly see Buddha, insight, and nirvana,
> These three are one—really they have no difference.
> The buddhas and bodhisattvas can benefit everyone:
> Insight is their mother, giving birth and nursing them.
> Since Buddha is a father to all beings,
> And insight gives birth to buddhas,
> It is therefore the grandmother of all living beings.
> Insight is one reality,

But Buddha speaks of it in various terms,
Using different words according to people's capacities.
If people see insight, they no longer want to dispute;
It is like the dew drying up all at once when the sun comes out.

COMMENTARY

Many different terms are used for insight, as well as for other elements
of Buddhism, in order to communicate with people of different cultures, mentalities, and capacities. Superficial followers may dispute
with each other about the terms they like, or split hairs about subjective senses of nuance, but those who actually awaken insight have no
such inclination any longer. For the insightful, the words and teachings were means of "crossing over" the mire of imprisoned thought;
once they have been put into effect and insight comes alive, the words
themselves are not the point. There is nothing more to argue about in
the light of insight, because no subjective projection is imposed on
reality, so truth is self-evident.

The power of insight can move two kinds of people;
The ignorant are afraid, the knowing rejoice.

COMMENTARY

The ignorant are afraid of insight because they fear that their cher-
ished opinions and beliefs will be threatened, thereby threatening the
stability of their worldview and sense of self. The knowing rejoice
because they realize that the dismantling or melting of rigid fixations
does not destroy the integrity of the self or the world but introduces
a realm of constructive freedom of choice. It may also be said that the
"ignorant," or "foolish," who are afraid of insight includes those who
are weak-willed and shrink from the responsibilities inherent in freedom of any kind.

If people attain insight, they become insightful;
They are not obsessed even with insight,
Let alone other things!

COMMENTARY

Obsession with insight before it is realized interferes with realization of insight. Obsession with insight on its realization interferes with complete integration of the mind. In Zen poetry, obsession with insight is pictured as being dazzled by a light shining right in your eyes, making you lose your way home.

> Insight comes from nowhere, and also goes nowhere;
> The intelligent may search everywhere
> But cannot find it anywhere.

COMMENTARY

Perfect insight is not a concept, notion, idea, or mental construction; therefore the intellect cannot apprehend it; direct insight and discursive intellect are different modalities of consciousness.

> If they don't see insight, this is called being bound;
> If people see insight, this too is called being bound.

COMMENTARY

Without insight, the mind is bound to its own constructions as it projects them onto reality at large. On the other hand, if "insight" is objectified, or reified, then the mind is bound by this objectification or reification of insight.

> If people see insight, this is attaining liberation;
> If they don't see insight, they also attain liberation.

COMMENTARY

Insight liberates the mind from the prison of frozen attention, fixated perceptions, and rigid habits of thought. Having deconstructed everything, insight itself does not stand; this is "not seeing insight" in a higher sense, going "beyond the beyond," to become liberated even from the notion of liberation.

This fact is quite marvelous, extremely deep, and very significant.
It is like a magical object, which you see though it cannot be seen.

COMMENTARY

A magical object is an illusion, which appears to be there yet is not
really there as perceived; therefore you can "see" it even though it
"cannot be seen." This is a common simile for the three natures of
things. The illusory appearance is the conceptualized, imagined, or
"nonexistent" nature. The props used to create the illusion constitute
the dependent, relative, or conditional nature. The fact that the object
apparently perceived in the illusion is not really there in the underlying props is the perfect or real nature. This analysis is applied not only
to mundane things but also to transcendental things; as will be seen
below, the entire structure of "Buddhism" per se is ultimately deconstructed in the path of perfect insight.

> The buddhas and bodhisattvas,
> The hearers and individual illuminates,
> Liberation, nirvana, and the Way,
> Are all realized through insight.

COMMENTARY

Speaking in terms of the two or five kinds of insight defined previously, it can be said that from the point of view of Mahayana Buddhism, the insight that is common to buddhas, bodhisattvas, hearers,
and individual illuminates—people of different levels of realization—is
the fundamental insight into the real nature of things. In this sense,
the teaching that specializes in perfect insight is referred to as the
Common Teaching in the classification of Tiantai Buddhism, which
integrates all the exoteric teachings but relies heavily on perfect insight teachings for metaphysics and meditation.

COMMENTARY

Granted that there is no difference or duality in the essential nature of
the primal insight that is common to all the levels of enlightenment,

the key point to realize is that insight plays a different role in the overall balance of each level. Even if the insight of one might be said to be deeper or vaster than another in some sense, yet that does not actually refer to insight per se but rather to the different measures and modes of cooperation of insight with other elements of enlightenment.

They speak in conventional terms for the world
Out of compassion for everyone,
Explaining things in provisional terms,
Not explaining even as they explain.

COMMENTARY

The Taoist classic *Tao-te Ching* says, "Ways can be articulated, but not a fixed path; names can be designated, but not fixed terms." Mahayana Buddhist teaching emphasizes the conventional and provisional nature of spoken teachings so that people will not quibble over external superficialities but use the words to direct their minds to the very heart of the matter. To explain without explaining means to use explanation as a means to something else, not as an end in itself. Religion is often associated, even unconsciously, with the holding and promulgating of certain doctrines, associated with specific verbal formulations. As noted earlier, this is what people argue and fight about; insight does not support this sort of religious or philosophical controversy.

It is in this sense that Buddha is said to have claimed at the end of his career that he had not said anything at all in forty-nine years. Zen classics take this to mean Buddha himself, the enlightened one, did not set up any dogma; that was done later by people who tried to make the teaching into an object. As an object it could be venerated, possessed, bartered, sold, usurped, and so on; and people did it all to the memory of Buddha and his teaching, just as people have done to the memories of all spiritual giants and teachings of ancient times. The Buddhist teaching of perfect insight was projected to get people beyond this stage of attachment to traces in the name of religion. And that, after all, is the very reason why the teaching of perfect insight makes no sense in itself insofar as it appears to be a series of negations.

> Perfect insight is like a bonfire,
> Ungraspable from the four directions.

COMMENTARY

The image of the bonfire represents ungraspability of insight by means of ordinary habitual thought processes. The four directions are the premises of existence, nonexistence, neither, and both. If the mental set with which one approaches anything, even insight, is rooted in presumptions that things as they seem or as they are conceived actually exist, or are totally nonexistent, or are neither there nor not there, or are both there and not there, it is deviated by that bias from the straight path of direct insight. Just as insects can alight anywhere except in a fire, it is said, so the human mind can cling anywhere except to perfect insight.

> No grasping is not even grasped—
> All grasping is relinquished.
> This is called the ungraspable—
> To grasp the ungraspable
> Is called getting a grasp.

COMMENTARY

The classical Zen master Baizhang said that the totality of the teachings is in three phases: first comes detachment, then detachment from detachment, then not even entertaining an understanding of not dwelling in detachment. He also said that the practice of perfect insight in Zen is nonseeking; but then if one seeks nonseeking, that is seeking. In the same way, if one hears of nongrasping and then grasps a rigid, absolutized concept of nongrasping, by following that notion religiously one could become too passive, possibly becoming irreversibly weak-willed or else aggressively nihilistic. Nongrasping is a door to a wider world, so to speak, not a world in itself. Once the door is opened and you go through it, the matter at hand is the wider world.

Insight has no destruction;
It is beyond all words and speech.
Wherever it goes, it does not abide—
Who can sing its merits?

2.

QUESTION: Why is perfect insight alone called great, not the other five perfections?

ANSWER: Because it can reach the other shore of the ocean of knowledge, reaching the end of all knowledge and fathoming its extreme limit; therefore it is called perfect, meaning that it reaches the other shore, or ultimate end.

As for greatness, the buddhas are the greatest in all worlds and all times; next are bodhisattvas, individual illuminates, and hearers. These four kinds of great people are all born from perfect insight, so it is called great.

Also, it can give people a great reward as a result, which is measureless and inexhaustible, permanent and unchanging, namely nirvana. The other five perfections cannot do this. Giving and the other perfections, without perfection of insight, can only give worldly rewards as results, so they cannot be called great.

COMMENTARY

The five perfections preliminary to insight are giving, morality, tolerance, diligence, and meditation. Without perfect insight, these five other perfections, even meditation, remain mundane practices, bounded by the limits of subjectivity. As the text says, the first five perfections without perfect insight can give only worldly rewards; in fact, under these conditions the results or "rewards" of trying to practice giving, morality, tolerance, diligence, and meditation without insight may very well be negative.

3.

QUESTION: What is knowledge?

ANSWER: Perfect insight is so because it encompasses all knowledge. How is that? As bodhisattvas seek buddhahood, they should study all principles and gain all knowledge—that is the knowledge of hearers, individual illuminates, and buddhas. These knowledges are of three kinds: learned, unlearned, and neither learned nor unlearned.

Knowledge that is neither learned nor unlearned is like the stage of dry intelligence—impurity, following the breathing, the bonds of the realm of desire, the four points of mindfulness, the state of warming, the state of peaking, the state of tolerance, the highest state in the world, and so on.

COMMENTARY

The stage of dry intelligence represents gaining intellectual understanding of Buddhism without yet having realized true emptiness.

Impurity refers to contemplation of impurities such as of the physical body, an elementary exercise to cultivate detachment from gross sensuality.

Following the breathing is a concentration exercise designed to cultivate concentration.

The bonds of the realm of desire refer to the practice of analyzing psychological bondage due to craving.

The four points of mindfulness are a contemplative exercise for detaching fixations of attention; they consist of mindfulness of the body as impure, mindfulness of sensation as irritating, mindfulness of inconstancy of mind, and mindfulness of phenomena as having no inherent identity.

The state of warming is a threshold of knowledge. Attainment of knowledge is likened to producing fire with a drill; "warming" is a stage before the "fire" ignites, when hardened fixations of mental habit soften and the mind begins to open.

The state of peaking is when contemplation becomes clearer and clearer, so that it is as if one were on the peak of a mountain, able to see all around.

The state of tolerance refers to recognition and acceptance of the facts of suffering, its origin, its cessation, and the path to the cessation of suffering.

The highest state in the world refers to the most refined and elevated state of mind that can be achieved short of realization of the noumenon. Because it is still prior to realization of the noumenon, this state is still "in the world" and not yet transcendental.

Knowledge that is learned includes knowledge, acceptance, and insight into the facts of suffering, all the way up to the insight of the adamantine samadhi of arhats on the ninefold path without obstacle.

Arhats are Buddhist saints who attain nirvana; adamantine samadhi is unbreakable absorption. The ninefold path without obstacle refers to contemplative deconstruction of the confusions of the realms of desire, form, and formlessness. The nine stages of this path consist of the realm of desire, four stages of meditation in the realm of form, and four stages of absorption in the realm of formlessness. The practitioner successively deconstructs confusion in each of these ascending states, so this path is said to be without obstacle.

Unlearned knowledge is all knowledge without learning from the arhat's ninth liberation knowledge, like the knowledge of ending, knowledge of nonoccurrence, and so on. Seeing the knowledge of the path of individual illuminates is also like this.

Liberation knowledge comes after confusion and delusion have been decisively terminated. The "ninth" liberation knowledge refers to the final of nine steps of successive liberation from the confusions and delusions of the realms of desire, form, and formlessness, as noted above.

Knowledge of ending, elsewhere called terminal knowledge, refers to the awareness consequent upon the ending of delusion, and it is also said to imply realization that there is no more regeneration of delusion. Knowledge of nonoccurrence, which is known by various names, is based on the realization that there is no definitive beginning to anything, only a continuum of interdependence within which we define time, space, and phenomena for the purposes of negotiating our way through this inconceivable infinity. Knowledge of nonoccurrence is also said to imply awareness of no further compulsion to become emotionally or intellectually bound to any of the realms that can be mentally construed from the ocean of perceptual possibilities.

4.

QUESTION: If the path of individual illuminates is also like this, how do you distinguish hearers from individual illuminates?

COMMENTARY

Hearers, or listeners, are those who follow a teaching or path to liberation offered them by a buddha, someone who is already enlightened. Individual illuminates are those who find a path to liberation on their own by objective observation of things as they are. The following explanation of the distinction is based on the understanding of emptiness.

> ANSWER: Though the path is of one kind, the uses of knowledge differ. Within true emptiness there is absorption in the emptiness of emptiness. Falsely viewed emptiness may have emptiness, but it has no absorption in the emptiness of emptiness.

The emptiness of emptiness means that emptiness itself is empty. That does not mean empty as in physically empty, but its emptiness means emptiness is not itself a thing. Easy enough to understand intellectually, this has nevertheless remained a contemplative trap throughout the ages, often mentioned in technical works on meditation. Falsely viewed emptiness that has emptiness without absorption in the emptiness of emptiness is what leads to dissociation. Because unmitigated dissociation would be fatal, deviated meditators who have strayed into false emptiness and survived are often found surrounded, or rather enclosed, by correspondingly hardened shells of external observances and fetishes, including dogmatic precepts and doctrines as well as personal uptightness.

The Fourth Grand Master of Zen said, "A bodhisattva in the beginning stage first realizes that all is empty. Subsequently one realizes that all is not empty. This is nondiscriminatory knowledge. It is the meaning of the saying that 'form itself is empty.' It is not emptiness resulting from annihilation of form; it means the very essence of form is empty. The practice of bodhisattvas has emptiness as its realization, but when beginning students see emptiness, this is *seeing* emptiness, not real emptiness. Those who cultivate the path to the point where they attain real emptiness do not see emptiness or nonemptiness—they have no views."

5.

People who see into true emptiness have previously practiced immeasurable charity, discipline, and concentrated meditation, so their hearts are soft and their bonds and compulsions are slight. After getting to be like this they attain true emptiness. In a false view of emptiness there is no such thing—there is only the desire to grasp emptiness with the mind warped by subjective thought and imagination.

COMMENTARY

This is a most important passage, worth reflecting on repeatedly in the quest for mental balance. On one level, it documents the fact that dissociated Buddhism has been repudiated all along in the classics, and engaged Buddhism is nothing new. The quintessential difference between those who see into true emptiness and those who only have subjective desires to grasp emptiness lies in the element of greed. Folly and aggression, the other main characteristics found among false seekers, seem to follow from greed. Those who realize emptiness are those who do not bring their greed into play in this domain of endeavor, whether it be their greed to be magically liberated from problems they should face and work through, or greed to be magically turned into a "master" who can have worshipers, or greed to have "enlightenment" conform to whatever one happens to think or imagine it may be. This is much emphasized in Zen lore, where it is said that the majority of devotees who reach it succumb to false emptiness—"The even ground is littered with skulls; those who get through the brambles are the masters."

6.

Suppose a bumpkin who does not know what salt is sees people putting salt on various meats and vegetables and eating them. He asks why they do that, and they tell him that salt can enhance the flavor of foods. Now the man thinks that if salt can make other things taste better, then its own flavor must be great. So he scoops up all the salt and eats a whole mouthful of it. The salty bitterness hurts his mouth, so he asks, "Why did you say salt improves flavor?"

The people say to him, "Fool! You have to adjust the amount and add it to food to enhance the flavor—how can you eat pure salt?!"

Ignorant people who hear of the door of liberation through emptiness do not practice virtues; they only want to attain emptiness. This is a false view that cuts off all roots of goodness.

COMMENTARY

This amusing story is told to illustrate and help us keep in mind the foregoing points about true and false emptiness, and it also shows the difference between alienated and engaged Buddhism. Please register and remember this story even if you register or remember nothing else in this book, because it can help you avoid a fundamental misconception of Buddhism and a fundamental futility in mental exercise. The great Buddhist master Nagarjuna, known for his works on emptiness and insight, and to whom this treatise is attributed, also wrote, "Emptiness wrongly viewed destroys the weak-minded, like a snake wrongly held or a mystic spell wrongly performed."

7.

The power of perfect insight is unobstructed by anything. If you go into the Abhidharma without having perfect insight, you will fall into existence; if you go into the doctrine of emptiness, you will fall into nonexistence.

COMMENTARY

"The Abhidharma" refers to works dealing with analysis of elements. To go into the Abhidharma way of thinking without penetrating insight conditions the mind to the notion of the elements as actually existing. On the other hand, to go into the teaching of emptiness without penetrating insight conditions the mind to dissociation or nihilism. Insight undermines the reification or absolutization of views of existence, emptiness, or any permutation thereof.

8.

When bodhisattva-mahasattvas employing perfect insight know the oneness of all things, they are also cognizant of the diversity of things. Though they know the diversity of things, they also know the oneness of things. This knowledge of bodhisattvas is called perfect insight.

COMMENTARY

The Zen classic *Blue Cliff Record* says, "In one there are many kinds; in two there is no duality." If you can only see everything as one and cannot see differences among things, this paralyzes you and makes you ineffective, unable to focus your mind or orient yourself. If you can only see everything as different and cannot see the totality, this makes it impossible for you to perceive the total context of events, rendering your comprehension fragmentary and your judgment partial. The Buddhist way is to integrate both aspects of consciousness or modes of thought, totalizing and particularizing, holistic and sequential, in a harmonious complementarity.

9.

QUESTION: How do bodhisattvas know the diversity of things? How do they know the unity of things?

ANSWER: Bodhisattvas view all things as one in terms of being one form, namely the form of being. Based on this there is mind in everything producing all this being.

This view of all things as one, practicing by viewing everything in terms of being itself rather than in terms of specific characteristics per se, is a temporary exercise for the purpose of detaching the mind from fixation on objects. There is a traditional Zen exercise designed to first focus the mind on oneness and then break through this standpoint— "All things return to One; where does the One return?"

QUESTION: How can there be mind arising where nothing exists?

ANSWER: If you say there is no such thing, that itself exists.

———————

Denial implies affirmation; if you try to deny something, whether metaphysically or psychologically, that implies recognition of its existence, whether potential or actual. This is why effort to detach from something may actually strengthen attachment, even if the attachment takes the form of rejection or repulsion.

10.

QUESTION: If the nature of all things is true emptiness, why differentiate diverse terminology for things? Why not speak only of true emptiness?

ANSWER: Bodhisattva-mahasattvas do not say emptiness is to be grasped or fixated upon. Were it to be grasped or fixated upon, they would not speak of the various different characteristics of things.

The emptiness of ungraspability has no obstruction. Were there obstruction, it would be graspable, not the emptiness of ungraspability. If bodhisattvas know the emptiness of ungraspability, they can still distinguish things out of compassion for people, to liberate them. This is the power of perfect insight.

Realization of emptiness by realization of ungraspability, being initially accomplished by mental examination and penetration of things and not by blanking the mind or dissociating from actuality, does not interfere with ordinary powers of perception. Fixation on emptiness, or obsession with emptiness, whether abstract or concrete, is like the case of the ignoramus in the story who eats a mouthful of salt after hearing that it enhances flavor. Not only does that fail to liberate the mind, it actually impedes spiritual growth and handicaps the individual in ordinary life.

11.

By means of meditation and concentration you break through distraction and become detached from illegitimate enjoyment of the desires of the five senses, so you are able to explain desirelessness to people. Meditation is the basis of perfect insight; perfect insight naturally occurs based on this meditation, as it says in scripture: "Single-minded concentration can see the real aspect of all things."

COMMENTARY

Illegitimate enjoyment of the desires of the five senses means obsessive attitudes toward pleasures, such as foster compulsive behavior that ultimately results in harm to oneself and others. Legitimate enjoyment of the desires of the five senses is part of the mechanism of life maintenance. One of the functions of tactical detachment is to gain a more objective perspective on the function of desires so as to enable the individual to make practical distinctions between legitimate and illegitimate enjoyment of sense desires. Meditation, concentration, and unification of mind, appropriately oriented, are means of acquiring detachment and objectivity.

12.

In the realm of desires, it is mostly the faulty actions of stinginess and greed that close the doors of goodness. When you practice perfect charity, you break through stinginess and greed, opening the doors of goodness.

Because you want to keep those doors open, you practice good ways. Then, because perfect conduct without meditation, concentration, and insight is still not apart from desire, you practice resignation. Knowing that while charity, good conduct, and resignation can open the doors of felicity, you also know that the resulting rewards of felicitous virtue are impermanent. After experiencing happiness, you fall into misery again. Weary of this impermanent felicity, you seek perfect insight into reality. How do you realize it? You have to be single-minded to realize it.

COMMENTARY

The limitations of good deeds and good conduct without insight and knowledge are also emphasized in Zen lore, to forestall self-righteous concentration on subjective notions of goodness, and also to undermine the factor of greed in subconscious expectations of good results from good deeds. The great master Muso Kokushi, national teacher of Japan, explained the psychological pitfall in overemphasis on temporal virtues without adequate insight: "Virtue without wisdom is said to be an enemy for three lifetimes. When the time is passed in ignorance doing only contaminated good, or virtue in hopes of reward, that makes it impossible to clarify the true ground of mind. This is the enemy of the first lifetime.

"Pleasurable states may eventually develop as a result of contaminated virtue. These are still in the realm of emotion, and they may occasion deepening of mundane attachments. These attachments become influences toward greedy and possessive behavior. This is the enemy of the second lifetime.

"When the pleasurable states are worn out, while the force of ignorance has not been diminished but rather increased by habitual attachment to the rewards of virtue, the fall from the state of elevation of feeling produces negative reactions. This is the enemy of the third lifetime." (Dream Conversations on Buddhism and Zen)

13.

Scripture: If bodhisattva-mahasattvas want to practice perfect charity, perfect conduct, perfect tolerance, perfect diligence, and perfect meditation, they should learn perfect insight.

TREATISE

QUESTION: If they are different, why does it say that those who want to practice perfect charity should learn perfect insight?

ANSWER: They are both same and different. The difference is that perfect insight refers to seeing the real aspect of all things, as it does not grasp or cling to anything. Charity means relinquishing all possessions, internal and external. When you practice charity with perfect insight, then the charity can be called perfect.

The first five perfections plant good qualities; perfect insight gets rid of obsessiveness and false views. It is like one worker planting grain and another worker removing weeds so the grain can grow and fruit.

COMMENTARY

Again the treatise presents easily remembered imagery to help maintain mindfulness of the need for balance in the overall development of the human being. Insight without charity fails to benefit the world by default; charity without insight fails to benefit the world by defect. The same is true of the relationship between insight and the other virtues of the first five perfections, or ways of transcendence.

QUESTION: Why is it necessary to learn perfect insight to practice perfect charity?

ANSWER: There are two kinds of charity, pure and impure. Impure charity includes charity given out of pride, with the thought "Others who are inferior to me give charity, so why can't I?"

Then there is charity given out of jealousy, with the

thought "My enemies have gotten reputations for charity, surpassing me in this way; now I should give a lot of charity to outdo them."

Then there is charity out of greed for reward, with the thought "If I give a little bit, I'll be rewarded a millionfold, so I'll give charity."

Then there is charity for repute, with the thought "If I take to giving charity, I will be trusted by others, and good people will count me as one of them."

Then there is charity for taking people in, with the thought "The people to whom I am giving charity will give me their allegiance."

Charity given with all sorts of complications like this is called impure charity. Pure charity has no such complications; it is just a matter of trusting in cause and effect with pure heart, having respect and compassion for those who receive charity, and not seeking present profit but only considering it merit for the afterlife. There is also pure charity that is not even given for benefit in the afterlife but just to cultivate the mind and help it seek nirvana.

There is also pure charity given with universal compassion, for the sake of others, not for one's own advantage in rapid attainment of nirvana, but only for supreme perfect enlightenment. This is called pure charity, because it has perfect insight at heart.

COMMENTARY

Charity complicated by pride or jealousy, or desire for reward, reputation, or influence over others, is really a form of commerce, or profiteering, the antithesis of charity. Buddhism does not recommend this sort of transactional charity, on the grounds that it tends to inflate the ego and interfere with enlightenment.

14.

Without perfect insight, the other five perfections cannot be called perfections. Just as a group of blind men cannot get where they are going without a guide, perfect insight leads the other five perfections to all-knowledge.

Perfect insight diffuses blind attachment to formal notions of practice and their subconscious use to inflate the ego and rationalize one's behavior: "Here is me being generous. Here is me being good. Here is me being tolerant. Here is me being diligent. Here is me meditating. Here is me being wise. This and this alone is charity. This and this alone is morality. This and this alone is tolerance. This and this alone is diligence. This and this alone is meditation. This and this alone is wisdom." Perfect insight silences these hidden conceits and prevents the mind from being captured by fixations of abstract and unreal ideas about what these virtues mean and how they can be put into practice.

15.

Scripture: If you want to know the suchness, true nature, and ultimate reality of all things, learn perfect insight.

TREATISE

There are two kinds of suchness of things. One is the particular individual aspect, the other is the absolute or real aspect.

The particular individual aspect is like the firmness of earth, the wetness of water, the heat of fire, the movement of wind. When you distinguish things like this, each has its own individual characteristics.

As for the absolute or real aspect, when you seek imaginatively in the individual aspects of things, absolute reality cannot be found.

This is an exercise in simultaneous perception of the particular and the universal, or multiplicity and unity. Both of these modes of perception,

in mutual cooperation, are essential to a round and balanced consciousness. The order of this exercise is opposite that of versions of
the same type of exercise illustrated earlier. Here the attention is first
focused on the particular individual aspects of things. After that the
attention is focused on the discrepancy between subjective imagination and objective reality, particularly the inherent incapacity of the
former to connect with the latter. This is intended to produce the
degree of detachment from imagined reality needed to perceive *suchness*, or things as they are.

16.

Scripture: Buddha said, "When bodhisattva-mahasattvas practice
charity with perfect insight, by the power of insightful skill in
means they are able to fulfill perfect charity, perfect conduct,
perfect patience, perfect diligence, perfect meditation, and
perfect insight."

Shariputra asked the Buddha how this is so. Buddha replied,
"Because giver, receiver, and gift cannot be grasped, they can
fulfill perfect charity. Because guilt and innocence cannot be
grasped, they can fulfill perfect morality. Because their minds
are unmoved, they fulfill perfect tolerance. Because their bodies and minds are energetic and they are not lazy, they fulfill
perfect diligence. Because they are not confused or blinded,
they fulfill perfect meditation. Because they know all things
are ungraspable, they fulfill perfect insight."

COMMENTARY

"Giver, receiver, and gift cannot be grasped" means that one who
knows the nature of things as they really are cannot feel pious or proud
about giving charity, cannot look down upon or expect anything in
return from anyone to whom anything is given, and cannot feel any
sense of personal cost or loss at having given a gift.

Innocence and guilt are relative, not absolute. One who kills an armed intruder to protect one's family is not guilty of the same kind of murder as one who kills a person for the purpose of robbery, or one who kills a person from anger or pride. A prostitute who steals from her pimp is not guilty of the same sort of theft as the pimp who steals from the prostitute. Someone who lies to the police to protect an innocent person is not guilty of the same dishonesty as one who lies to the police to shield the guilty or one who lies to the police to indict the innocent. These are extreme examples, but they illustrate the reality that insight is key to understanding the relative nature of morality and how good and bad depend on a changeable nexus of conditions. All who have studied history, of course, are well aware of warfare, torture, and murder carried out in the name of promoting good and opposing evil. That should be a clue to the significance, in this domain, of the possibility of a transcendental insight that is impartial and unaffected by personal, national, historical, and cultural conditioning. Of course, it may be that people tend to think their own values are themselves the ones that are universal, unbiased, and objective. Part of the task of the Buddhist path is to examine, from ordinarily unexamined various points of view, whether or not, or to what extent values may really be objective or universal.

If notions embodying hostility and hatred are deeply rooted in the patterns of inherited and ingrained attitudes, yet the feelings are formally suppressed in the name of tolerance, the peace that may bring will tend to be fragile, and what is suppressed may unavoidably surface. What is most unfortunate is that negative emotions that have been forcibly suppressed in the name of tolerance may erupt at precisely those times when real tolerance is most necessary and useful in human affairs. That is why the spontaneous balance and mental stability resulting from perfect insight, depicted as the mind being unmoved, is quintessential for the perfection of tolerance.

Perfect insight does not act upon anything or withdraw from anything, and does not get into emotional or intellectual complications about anything. Therefore it saves both mental and physical energy. Persistent saving of energy leads to energization and empowerment, felt both mentally and physically.

Some Zen masters have made a particular point of this practice of saving energy. The great Dahui (Ta Hui) wrote, "While you are paying attention, you should not make any effort to struggle with whatever is going on in your mind. While struggling you waste energy. As the Third Grand Master of Zen said, 'If you try to stop movement and return to stillness, the attempt to be still will increase movement.' When you notice that you are saving energy in the midst of the mundane stress of daily affairs, this is where you gain energy." (*Zen Essence: The Science of Freedom*)

Zen master Foyan said, "Generally speaking, practical application of Zen requires detachment from thoughts. This method of Zen saves the most energy. It just requires you to detach from emotional thoughts and understand that there is nothing concrete in the realms of desire, form, and formlessness. Only then can you apply Zen practically. If you try to practice it otherwise, it will seem bitterly painful by comparison." (*Instant Zen: Waking Up in the Present*)

17.

If bodhisattva-mahasattvas want to reach the other shore of both compounded and uncompounded things, they should learn perfect insight.

COMMENTARY

"Compounded things" refers to all ordinary phenomena, as they are compounded of particles and elements. "Uncompounded things" refers to space, nirvana realized by analysis, and nonanalytic nirvana; some accounts also include stability, obliteration of the senses, and suchness in this category. Compounded and uncompounded things are also called created and uncreated things. The *Sandhinirmocana-sutra* illustrates insight reaching the other shore of both compounded and uncompounded things with great clarity: "'Created' is an artificial definition temporarily set up by the Buddha. As such, it is a verbal expression assembled by conceptualization. If it is a verbal expression assembled by conceptualization, ultimately it is a verbal expression of various conceptualizations, and not actually real. Therefore it is not created. If you say it is uncreated, this too comes down to a matter of words. If you talk about anything outside of the created and the uncreated, the same thing applies. That does not mean, however, that there is nothing being discussed. What is that thing? Sages, with their knowledge and vision, detach from names and words and therefore actualize enlightenment. Then, because they wish to make others aware of this nature that is beyond words, they temporarily set up names and characteristics and call something created. 'Uncreated' is also an artificial definition temporarily set up by the Buddha. As such, it is a verbal expression assembled by conceptualization, which means that it is ultimately verbal expression of various conceptualizations and so is not actually real. Therefore it is not uncreated. If you say it is created, this too comes down to a matter of words. Even if you talk about anything outside of the created and the uncreated, the same thing applies. That does not mean, however, that there is nothing being discussed. What is the thing? Sages, with their knowledge and vision, detach from names and words and therefore actualize enlightenment. Then, because they want to make others aware of this nature beyond words, they temporarily set up names and characteristics and call something uncreated." (*Buddhist Yoga*)

18.

If bodhisattva-mahasattvas want to know the suchness, characteristics, and realm of nonoccurrence of all things past, present, and future, they should learn perfect insight.

COMMENTARY

Suchness is the direct witness of all things without conceptual mediation or representation; insofar as there is no internal verbalization or description, things as so witnessed are simply said to be *thus* or *such*, and their being-so is called *thusness* or *suchness*. Characteristics refer to the specific features of individual things. The realm of nonoccurrence refers to the sense in which there is no absolute beginning of anything, insofar as everything is part of an all-encompassing nexus of interacting and interdependent conditions and nothing exists in and of itself. Knowledge of the realm of nonoccurrence enables the mind to cognize both suchness and characteristics at the same time, without confusion. Thus perfect insight is considered key to both holistic and particularizing modes of knowing.

19.

If bodhisattva-mahasattvas want to avoid stinginess, immorality, anger, laziness, distraction, and folly, let them learn perfect insight.

COMMENTARY

Conventional religious pietists will try to eliminate these negative personality elements by defining and identifying them in certain behaviors and then attempting to rule out those behaviors and suppress them. This may achieve a degree of inhibition but does not reach the stage of avoidance, wherein the individual sees through the psychological mechanisms underlying these negative elements and is mentally enabled, by this direct penetrating insight, to remain essentially outside the range of their compulsive influences.

Zen master Bunan said, "It is easy to refrain from approaching things; it is harder to be inaccessible to things." Ordinary discipline at its best manages to refrain from approaching blameworthy things, whether in one's own personality and behavior or in the world at large; the discipline of perfect insight is to be inwardly inaccessible to these thoughts and things.

Scripture on Perfect Insight for Benevolent Rulers

❧❧

1.

King Prasenajit asked Buddha, "How do all bodhisattvas preserve buddhahood? How do they preserve the conditions for the practices of the ten stages?"

Buddha said, "When bodhisattvas teach, they do not look upon the suchness of form; or upon the suchness of sensation, cognition, conditionings, or consciousness; or upon the suchness of beings, self, others, permanence, pleasure, identity, or purity; or upon the suchness of knowledge, or liver of life; or upon the suchness of bodhisattvas; or upon the suchness of the six perfections, the four integrative methods, or all practices; or upon the suchness of the two truths.

"Therefore the nature of all things is in absolute reality empty—it does not come or go, it has no origination or destruction. It is the same as absolute reality, equivalent to the essence of reality; none other, no different, like space.

"So the clusters, media, and elements have no self and no inherent characteristics. This constitutes the insight by which bodhisattvas practice and teach the ten stages."

COMMENTARY

Not looking upon the suchness of things may be understood on different levels, but both are important elements of practice. First, it means one does not think of the suchness of things: "This is the suchness of things" or "The suchness of things is thus and so." Second, it means that one does not abide in unmediated direct witness all the time, because that too would produce an imbalance in mentation.

Zen master Baizhang said, "To speak of mirroring awareness is still not really right. Discern the pure by way of the impure. If you say immediate mirroring awareness is correct, or that there is something else beyond mirroring awareness, this is all delusion. If you keep dwelling in immediate mirroring awareness, this too is the same as delusion. It is called the error of naturalism." (*The Five Houses of Zen*)

2.

The king said to Buddha, "If all things are so, then is bodhisattvas' protection and teaching of people actually teaching people?"

Buddha said, "O king, in terms of the essential nature, and form, sensation, cognition, conditionings, and consciousness, they do not dwell on form, nor do they dwell on denial of form; nor do they dwell on negation of denial of form. This also applies to sensation, cognition, conditionings, and consciousness—they do not dwell on any of them, nor do they not dwell on any of them.

COMMENTARY

Zen master Baizhang identified three phases of the Buddhist teachings as a whole, which are clearly represented here: Baizhang describes the first phase as detachment (here: not dwelling on form, and so on); the second phase is not dwelling in detachment (here: not dwelling "on denial of form"); and the third phase is not entertaining an understanding of nondwelling (here: not dwelling on negation of denial of form, and so on). Freedom is beyond these three stages. The application here is that when people with awakened insight help and guide others, they do not view other people in the same way that those other people view them, nor do they view other people the same way they view themselves. As will be seen below, however, that does not mean they do not see or know how other people view things, only that they do not entertain or make a living on such views themselves.

"Why? Because it is not the way form is, yet not not the way form is; but in the sense of conventional truth, on three conditions they are said to see people.

"In the sense that the nature of all things is real, the buddhas, seven grades of saints, and eight grades of sages on the Three Vehicles can be said to see; and so can those who hold the sixty-two views also be said to see.

"O king, if names are called seeing things, then the buddhas, those on the Three Vehicles, and all beings do not not see all things."

The Zen master Mazu said, "All living beings have always been absorbed in the nature of things. They are always within absorption in the nature of things, dressing, eating, conversing. The functions of the six senses, and indeed all activities, are all the nature of things."

The Zen master Dogen wrote, "Because the nature of things is oneself, it is not the self as misconceived by externalists or obsessives. In the nature of things there is no externalism or obsession; it is only eating breakfast, eating lunch, and having a snack. Even so, those who claim to have studied for a long time, even twenty or thirty years, pass their whole life in a daze when they read or hear talk of the nature of things. Those who claim to have fulfilled Zen study and assume the rank of teacher, while they hear the voice of the nature of things and see the forms of the nature of things, yet their body and mind, objective and subjective experience, always just rise and fall in the pit of confusion. What this is like is wrongly thinking that the nature of things will appear when the whole world we perceive is obliterated, that the nature of things is not the present totality of phenomena. The principle of the nature of things cannot be like this." (*Shobogenzo: Zen Essays by Dogen*)

3.

The king said to Buddha, "In terms of perfect insight, existing things are neither real nor unreal. How is this perceived in the Mahayana?"

The Buddha said, "Great king, the Mahayana sees neither reality nor unreality. If things are neither real nor unreal, this is called the emptiness of neither reality nor unreality. The very essence of things is empty: form, sensation, cognition, conditionings, and consciousness are empty; the twelve media and eighteen elements are empty; the six main constituents of being are empty; the four truths and twelve conditions are empty.

"These things occur, abide, and pass away immediately; they are simultaneously existent and empty. This is the way it is moment to moment—things occur, abide, and pass away immediately. Why? Ninety moments make an instant of thought; in one instant of thought, a moment occurs and dies out nine hundred times. All things, including matter, are like this."

COMMENTARY

The moment occurring and dying out nine hundred times means that a moment is defined as the length of nine hundred thought waves. Ninety of these moments make an instant, so there are eighty-one thousand thought waves in an instant. Naturally, this is not an absolute figure but an illustration for contemplative purposes. Nevertheless, although it is hard to say at this time in our knowledge of brain function that there is a specific figure or range that can be measured, nevertheless the principle of the speed of thought, or the brevity of thought waves, is sound. This is held to account for the seeming continuity of the world as we experience it in everyday consciousness. The contemplative use of the brevity of thought waves as a comparison for the constant flux of matter, sensation, cognition, mental formations, and consciousness is a classical way to the experience of nirvana earlier described as nirvana by way of analysis. This is cultivated nirvana.

"Because perfect insight is empty, it does not see objects and does not see the truths—all things are empty. Inside is empty, outside is empty, inside and outside are empty, compounded things are empty, uncompounded things are empty, origination is empty, essence is empty, ultimate truth is empty, perfect insight is empty, cause is empty, buddhahood is empty, and emptiness is empty; thus all are empty."

The previous paragraph describes the contemplative maneuver known as entering into emptiness by way of conditionality; this paragraph represents graduation from the process to the result, temporarily dwelling in vision of emptiness.

"It is just that things exist because of combination. Sensations exist because of combination. Causes exist because of combination. Effects exist because of combination. The ten practices therefore exist, buddhahood therefore exists, and so does every other state of being."

This paragraph describes the next maneuver after entering emptiness and dwelling in vision of emptiness, namely reentering the conditional from emptiness. This is the basis of compassion. Going back and forth along the route described by these three stages is a way to contemplative realization of the middle way, or the path of central balance. This "triple gate" is found throughout the Buddhist scriptures on perfect insight; this body of lore was made the basis of Tiantai meditation practice in China, Korea, and Japan. From Tiantai it entered into Zen, where it is evident from the era of the founding grand masters and is shown in Zen records to have been repeatedly reintroduced over the centuries. (*Stopping and Seeing*)

"Good man, if bodhisattvas see things, beings, self, others, or knowledge, these people are practicing worldly conventions and are no different from worldlings."

This is an example of scriptural parameters of enlightenment that enable the sincere and alert aspirant to differentiate between seemingly religious people and institutions that are in reality vehicles for worldly aspirations, and seemingly worldly people or establishments that are in reality vehicles for spiritual content.

"If you are unmoved in the midst of all things and do not reach for them, they have no forms yet are not formless. All things are thus, and so are the buddhas, their teachings, and their communities. This is being imbued with eighty-four thousand perfect insights in a single moment of consciousness in the first stage of enlightenment."

The first sentence of this paragraph is the "eye," or key guidance. To be unmoved in the midst of all things means not reacting automatically to things, either inwardly or outwardly, emotionally or intellectually. Not reaching for things means not obsessing, not grasping, not projecting wishes, fears, suppositions, and so on. Then things have no forms in the sense that one has no rigid fixations on things as one supposes, fears, or wishes them to be; yet things are not formless either, in that one who is not subject to distortions of thought can tell things apart from each other.

"This immediate conveyance is called the Mahayana or Great Vehicle; the immediate relief is called the vajra, or thunderbolt, and also called stabilization."

The method is called a conveyance or vehicle in the sense that it conducts the mind to the destination and is not to be made an object of fixation in itself. The conveyance is called immediate because in-sight can see directly when the mind is not affected by things and does not reach for things. The term *vajra* means thunderbolt or dia-mond, which represents insight smashing or cutting through false views; this is called immediate relief because it is the burden of these views that afflicts the confused mind.

4.

Buddha said, "Great king, if bodhisattvas see objects, see knowledge, see explanation, see reception, this is not enlight-ened seeing. They are seeing things with distorted concep-tions; they are ordinary people."

COMMENTARY

Seeing objects, knowledge, explanation, and reception refers to sub-consciously believing that things are as they appear, that description is knowledge, that repetition and elaboration of conventional descrip-tions is explanation, and that people can thereby understand truth and reality. These are said to be distorted conceptions insofar as they un-consciously mistake subjective notions for objective realities. Even if this is done in an overtly religious, philosophical, or spiritual context, the approach is still that of mundane convention and results in nothing more elevated than that.

5.

Well-aware bodhisattvas, as guardians of the four quarters, are simultaneously aware of both absolute and conventional realities; with impartial techniques of guidance they teach sen-tient beings, traversing a hundred countries, before they finally ascend to the formless path of the One Vehicle and enter nou-menal insight. This is called abiding. Abiding there, they de-velop virtuous conduct, so it is called a stage. In the first stage they single-mindedly fulfill virtuous conduct without budging from ultimate truth.

COMMENTARY

Guarding the four quarters means awakening impartial compassion. In the Five Ranks description of the path of enlightenment according to the *Lotus Sutra*, guardianship of the four quarters is the third rank. The meaning of this is more explicit in the Five Ranks of Zen outlining the interrelation of the absolute and relative, a teaching that seems to have derived from a synthesis of the Five Ranks of the *Lotus Sutra* with the Four Reality Realms of Flower Ornament Buddhism.

Zen master Hakuin explains this third rank, which in Zen is called coming from within the absolute, in simple pragmatic terms: "Enlightening beings of the higher vehicle do not dwell in the state of result they have realized; from the ocean of effortlessness they radiate unconditional great compassion. Riding on the four universal pure vows, turning the wheel of teaching, they seek enlightenment above while edifying people below." (*Kensho: The Heart of Zen*)

6.

Insight has no knowledge and no view: it does not act on anything, relate to anything, come from anything, or sense anything. It does not apprehend any form of perception. Therefore the form of practice of this path is like space. Since it is like this by virtue of its normal character, how can it be attained by mindfulness or mindlessness?

COMMENTARY

The *Heap of Jewels Scripture* says, "The embodiment of reality cannot be sought by means of perception or cognition. It is not what is seen by the physical eye because it has no form. It is not what is seen by the

celestial eye because it has no illusion. It is not what is seen by the eye
of wisdom because it is beyond attributes. It is not what is seen by the
objective eye because it is beyond all configurations. It is not what is
seen by the enlightened eye because it is beyond all modes of consciousness." Zen master Baizhang commented, "If one does not produce such views as these, this is called the vision of a buddha."

7.

The consciousness of living beings differs from wood or stone
from the initial moment of consciousness, which can produce
good or evil. Evil is the root of infinite evil consciousnesses;
good is the root of infinite good consciousnesses. From the
very first moment of awareness to the very last moment of
awareness, untold consciousnesses are produced, forming the
bodies and minds of living beings.

COMMENTARY

Reactions to impressions have effects, which are attributed to the impressions themselves, or to objectifications of the impressions, thought
to be the causes of everything that has happened. The buildup of habitual reactions to impressions conditions the characteristics of the
impressions habitually formed in the mind. These psychological and
behavioral habits, developed in the course of living from raw instinctual and acquired emotional and intellectual materials, formulate the
activity of body and mind, including those factors that are conducive
to physical and mental health and illness.

The *Avatamsaka-sutra* says, "Just as the magician's arts can make various
things appear, inconceivable is the number of realms due to the force
of beings' acts. Just like pictures drawn by an artist, so are all worlds
made by the painter-mind. Beings' physical differences arise from mental discriminations; thus are the lands varied, all depending on acts.
. . . Many lands are produced by the force of beings' acts, supported

by different atmospheres. The phenomena of the worlds are thus vari-
ously seen; yet they really have no origination and no disintegration.
In each moment of mind are infinite lands produced. By enlightened
spirituality all are seen as pure." (*The Flower Ornament Scripture*)

8.

Because the six consciousnesses of ordinary people are coarse,
they apprehend countless artificially defined material phenomena—blue, yellow, square, round, and so on. Because the six
consciousnesses of sages are pure, they apprehend all actual
material phenomena—actual color, form, scent, flavor, and
texture.

COMMENTARY

So-called ordinary people are those who apprehend things only as
they have been conditioned to perceive and recognize them. So-called
sages are those who can apprehend phenomena more directly, without
the restrictive intervention of preconceived notions. That is why sages
are said to see more, or more truly, than ordinary people usually do,
because their direct knowledge is not conditioned or limited or
warped by expectations or assumptions unconsciously based on hear-
say and unquestioned convention.

9.

Being and nonbeing are originally two, like the two horns of
an ox. While perceptive understanding sees nonduality, the
two truths are always nonidentical. The understanding mind
sees nonduality—it cannot find duality. This does not mean
that the two truths are one; if they were not two, how could
they be apprehended? In terms of understanding, they are always intrinsically one; in terms of truth, they are always inherently two. By thorough comprehension of this nonduality you
truly penetrate the ultimate truth.

The expression "two truths" is used to refer to relative and absolute, or temporal and ultimate truths. What is conventionally said to exist is conditional and therefore nonexistent in an absolute sense; things as we perceive them appear as they are relative to our senses, not as they are in themselves. In contemplation of relativity to enter into realization of emptiness, the mind goes from observation of relative phenomena to meditation on relativity itself, then from there to absorption in emptiness. In emergence from emptiness to reenter the relative world, the mind shifts its focus from essence to characteristics. Once emptiness has been experientially realized, the relativity of perceptual bias no longer interferes with intuitive insight into the absolute. This is what is called comprehension of nonduality. This is the manner of experience referred to in classical Zen teaching as being like space, or like the sky, containing the forms of everything but unattached to appearances.

10.

In worldly truth illusions occur like flowers in the sky, nonexistent as reflections or a third hand. Illusions seem to exist, because of causes and conditions; seeing illusory beings is called the fact of illusion. Magicians see that illusions do not exist in true reality; this is called the vision of all buddhas, and the vision of bodhisattvas too.

Flowers in the sky, reflections, and a third hand represent the so-called conceptualized nature of things, also referred to as the purely imagined nature, or the nonexistent nature. This is not an absolute nonexistence, in the sense that it does not mean nothing is there at all, but rather it refers to the nonexistence of absolute objective reality in the conceptualized or imagined nature of things as they seem or appear to be relative to our senses and intellects. This implies that the enlightened and enlightening do not necessarily take things at face value, yet they do not disregard how things seem, to themselves and to others. That is how they can be or become unaffected by automatically reactive thoughts and feelings about things themselves, by being or becoming aware of their possible range of effects on various mentalities or mental patterns unleavened by penetrating insight.

11.

Bodhisattva-mahasattvas always illumine two truths within oneness to teach people. Buddhas and living beings are one, not two, because living beings are empty; so it can be posited that enlightenment is empty. Because of the emptiness of enlightenment, it can be posited that living beings are empty.

COMMENTARY

Buddhism teaches that there is an original potential within us, called buddha nature, and a second nature, a habit nature that is partly inherited and partly acquired. The transcendental fact that the habit nature is not absolutely real, not our true identity, is called the emptiness of living beings. The everyday fact that the habit nature does exist mentally, and the fact that this existence is reflected in behavioral patterns that reconfirm the mental habit nature, make it necessary to resort to two truths in order to liberate the mind from excessive confinement to habit nature enough to open up conscious experience of original buddha nature. By penetrating the opacity of the habit nature with insight, one is said to realize that "living beings" are "empty," and in this way one is no longer mentally clouded by the habit nature and can see and act from within the buddha nature.

The buddha nature can operate in the same individual as the habit nature because the habit nature is not absolute or absolutely binding. This implies that enlightenment, or realization of buddha nature, is not a thing of any conceivable order of existence, for that notion would be another item subject to the mechanical processing of the habit nature. The emptiness of enlightenment means freedom from preconceived notions, which implies that the habit nature does not overrule. This is represented as the emptiness of living beings, which also implies that people are not necessarily doomed to the limitations of their habit nature but can become liberated from the tyranny of inherited and ingrained patterns of mental habit so that their buddha nature can rule over their secondary human nature.

12.

Because all things are empty, therefore emptiness is empty. Why? Because insight is formless; the two truths are empty, and insight is empty. From ignorance to omniscience, there is no sign of selfness or otherness. Therefore when the five eyes are complete, they see without seeing anything and do not grasp whether they operate or not, and do not grasp when neither operative nor inoperative; they do not grasp anything at all.

COMMENTARY

The emptiness of emptiness means that emptiness is not something in itself and cannot be objectified or grasped as an object. Since ancient times there have evidently been those who cultivate mental blankness, or "indefinite darkness," or a realm of clarity as a mental object, and call that emptiness. There are countless references to this pitfall in Zen lore.

———————————

The "five eyes" of the complete human potential are mentioned in the selection from the *Heap of Jewels* scripture cited above in the commentary on segment 6 of this group of selections. There is the physical eye, the celestial (clairvoyant) eye, the eye of wisdom, the objective eye, and the enlightened eye. To say that these five eyes see without seeing anything means, in the context of the two truths, that they see all that is relative to their perceptive capacities, but no perceptive capacity can make an object of the absolute or ultimate truth that is not relative to anything. Any object, or objectification, is already in the relative realm by dint of its very objectification relative to a perceptive or cognitive capacity. This is why the scriptural passage mentioned says that the embodiment of reality is beyond the scope of the five eyes.

13.

When bodhisattvas have not yet attained buddhahood, they make enlightenment into an affliction. When bodhisattvas attain buddhahood, they make afflictions into enlightenment. How so? By virtue of nonduality in ultimate truth, because the buddhas and all things are thus.

COMMENTARY

Making enlightenment into an affliction means making enlightenment into an object of desire on the ordinary plane. Making afflictions into enlightenment means becoming spiritually liberated by penetrating understanding of psychological complications.

———————

Zen master Muso quotes an old saying that illustrates this point and helps to keep it in mind for practical purposes: "If you get obsessed with Buddhism, then Buddhism is a worldly thing. If you are not obsessed with worldly things, then worldly things are Buddhist teachings."

14.

If bodhisattvas seeing living beings see unity or duality, they do not see unity and do not see duality. Unity and duality are the ultimate truth. Being and nonbeing are both conventional

truth. Three truths encompass all things—the truth of emptiness, the truth of matter, and the truth of mind.

COMMENTARY

The three truths can be understood in terms of the teaching device of
the three natures cited earlier. The truth of emptiness is the real or
perfect nature of things, the truth of matter is the relative or dependent nature of things, and the truth of mind is the conceptual, imaginary, or nonexistent nature of things.

15.

When the fire that ends the eon goes out, the whole universe
will be empty; the highest mountains and the deepest oceans
will all be reduced to ash. The fortunes of gods and spirits will
end there. Even yin and yang pass away; how can a country
endure? Birth, aging, sickness, death—they go on in cycles
unending. Facts are at variance with wishes; worry and sorrow
hurt. When desires are deep, troubles are heavy; ulcers don't
come from outside. The three worlds are all uncomfortable—
what can a nation rely on?

Existence originally is itself nonexistent; causes and conditions make it. What flourishes inevitably declines, what is solid
invariably dematerializes. Living beings, profuse as they are,
all are like illusory presences; sound and echo are both empty,
and so too are the nation and country.

The conscious spirit has no form; it temporarily rides on
four serpents. Ignorance takes care of it, so it thinks it's a pleasant ride. The physical body has no permanent host, and the
spirit has no permanent house; since even body and spirit part,
how can you own a nation?

COMMENTARY

This is a meditation on emptiness in terms of impermanence, used to
cultivate detachment from ambition, contentiousness, and possessive-

ness. Here it is addressed to kings of countries, that they might cease
to wage wars of conquest and annexation, cease to aggrandize themselves at the expense of others. It also applies, naturally, to the individual attitude toward self-government.

16.

Bodhisattvas in training practice the ten virtues, view every
part of their own body's earth, water, fire, air, ether, and consciousness as impure. Then they view the fourteen organs—
that is, five consciousnesses, five senses, male and female
organs, the organ of ideation, and the root of life—as having
innumerable faults. Because of this they develop a mind with
unexcelled roots of goodness.

As they constantly cultivate the thought that everything in
the three realms is impure, they attain the contemplative
method of recognizing impurity. Living in the house of Buddha, they practice the six harmonies—namely similar thought,
word, and deed; similar views; similar conduct; and similar studies. They practice eighty-four thousand paths of
perfection.

When they practice the ten virtues before learning tolerance, bodhisattvas may regress as well as progress, like hairs
blown this way and that in the wind.

COMMENTARY

"In training" signifies elementary practice, including charity and goodness combined with detachment, unselfishness, sociability, and dedica-
tion of all inner and outer experiences to the process of complete
enlightenment.

———————

At the stage where they are said to be "in training," the qualities they
cultivate are not yet developed to the point of spontaneity and natural-

ness, so people are not yet definitively stabilized and may as yet back-slide from time to time in the course of their spiritual evolution.

17.

Naturalized bodhisattvas practice ten insightful contempla-tions and extinguish ten delusions. Even self, others, and knowledge are unreal; whatever form, whatever sensation, whatever phenomenon, cannot be grasped. There are no fixed definitions, no identity or otherness. So when they observe the practice of emptiness contemplation, they also practice a million perfections.

COMMENTARY

The ten insightful contemplations are called the four points of mind-fulness, the three roots of goodness, and contemplation of the three times. The four points of mindfulness up to the experience of nirvana are mindfulness of the body as impure, mindfulness of sensation as irritating, mindfulness of mind as inconstant, and mindfulness of phe-nomena as having no inherent identity. After nirvana, the four points of mindfulness are mindfulness of the body as spacelike, mindfulness of sensation as neither inside nor outside, mindfulness of mind as un-graspable, and mindfulness of phenomena as neither good nor bad. The three roots of goodness are freedom from greed, freedom from hatred, and freedom from folly. The three times contemplated are past, present, and future.

The ten delusions are also called ten compulsions. They are divided into two categories, the acute and the dull. Greed, hatred, folly, con-ceit, and doubt are called the five dull compulsions. The notion of the body as real, extreme views, false views, views attached to opinions, and views attached to precepts and prohibitions are called the five acute compulsions.

18.

Bodhisattvas on the path abide in stable tolerance and view all things as having no origination, no abiding, and no destruction. That is to say the five senses, the three realms, and the two truths have no identity or otherness, because their essence is ungraspable as it really is.

COMMENTARY

Zen master Zhenjing said, "When you recognize illusion, you become detached, without performing any expedient techniques. When you detach from illusion, you become awake, without any gradual process."

––––––––––––––

Zen master Baizhang said, "When you realize that senses and objects fundamentally do not connect, you become liberated on the spot."

Key Teachings of the
Great Scripture on Perfect Insight

1.

When bodhisattva-mahasattvas practice perfect insight, they do not view emptiness, or accord or discord with emptiness. They do not view signlessness, or accord or discord with signlessness. They do not view wishlessness, or accord or discord with wishlessness.

Why? Because there is neither accord nor discord in emptiness, signlessness, and wishlessness. When bodhisattva-mahasattvas practice perfect insight, it is by virtue of accord with such truths that they are to be said to accord with perfect insight.

When bodhisattva-mahasattvas practicing perfect insight have penetrated the inherent emptiness of all things, they do not view matter in terms of accord or discord; they do not view sensation, cognition, conditionings, or consciousness in terms of accord or discord.

These bodhisattva-mahasattvas do not view the connection or disconnection of matter and the past. Why? Because they do not see the past. They do not view the connection or dis-

connection of sensation, cognition, conditionings, or consciousness with the past. Why? Because they do not see the
past.

They do not view the connection or disconnection of matter with the future. Why? Because they do not see the future.
They do not view the connection or disconnection of sensation, cognition, conditionings, or consciousness with the future. Why? Because they do not see the future.

They do not view the connection or disconnection of matter with the present. They do not view the connection or
disconnection of sensation, cognition, conditionings, or consciousness with the present. Why? Because they do not see the
present.

When bodhisattva-mahasattvas practice perfect insight,
they do not view the connection or disconnection of past and
future. They do not view the connection or disconnection of
past and present. They do not view the connection or disconnection of future and past. They do not view the connection
or disconnection of future and present. They do not view the
connection or disconnection of future with past and present.
They do not view the connection or disconnection of present
with past and future. They do not view the connection or disconnection of past, future, and present. Why? Because the
three times are empty.

When bodhisattva-mahasattvas practice perfect insight, by
connecting with these principles they are to be said to connect
with perfect insight.

COMMENTARY

Emptiness, signlessness, and wishlessness are called the three doors of
liberation. Emptiness is defined in eighteen ways in the major scripture
on perfect insight; those who no longer view emptiness, or accord or
discord with emptiness, are those who have already understood the
definitions and experienced their premises, consequently they have no
more need to dwell on descriptions of emptiness and are not obsessed
or inebriated with experiential vision of emptiness.

Signlessness means that the external appearances of things as apprehended by the senses are not the essential realities of things in themselves. All things are said to be signless or formless in essence because
their objective reality does not conform to our subjective descriptions
of their features as we relate to them. Those who no longer view signlessness are those who have disabused themselves of the unconscious
identification of descriptions of things with the things themselves,
who no longer need to dwell on the principle of signlessness, and
who do not objectify signlessness as something in itself, or cling to
amorphous nebulosity as realization of signlessness. They see that
signs or appearances themselves are not absolute defining marks; their
insight into signlessness does not obliterate appearances.

Wishlessness means that things in themselves do not have the intentions and designs we bring to our relationships with them. We may
think we are going in a certain direction in accord with conditions, we
may feel that circumstances seem to be taking us this way and so it is
natural to follow, when all along we are actually following an unconscious agenda whose suppositions we never pause to examine because
we have attributed the logic of the route to the force of events or
the meaning of life as we conceive of it. By dwelling for a time in
contemplation of the nature of things as in themselves innocent of our
purposes and designs, we can learn to better distinguish objective facts
from subjective projections and also see how our involvement affects
the course of events. Those who no longer view wishlessness, or accord or discord with wishlessness, are those who have clarified their
own minds in this respect and do not need the contemplation any
longer; to remain fixated on the notion of "wishlessness" would there-
after become morbid, producing a sense of meaninglessness rather
than liberation.

Past, present, and future are relative frameworks of reference. Today is
yesterday's tomorrow, and it is also tomorrow's yesterday—how we

view it depends on whether we are thinking of present circumstances as consequences of past events, or of future possibilities as outcomes of present choices. Something that happened in the past may still be happening today, in a continuity of process or a persistence of effects; something that may happen in the future can have an effect in the present, in the form of preoccupation with hopes and fears, and consequent thoughts and action. So if we simply think of something as only in the past, or still to come, or temporarily present, we may be ineffective in our understanding of our living heritage, for better or worse; of our present situation and what we could or should be doing; and of our potentiality and possibilities in the future, and what the actual consequences of our present acts will be.

While the "nonviewings" are posed in negative terms, when understood pragmatically in their total context, not ideologized separately based on word content, it can be seen that the aims and outcomes of these overtly deconstructive exercises in insight are actually positive.

2.

Bodhisattva-mahasattvas practicing perfect insight do not form this thought: "I am practicing perfect insight." They do not form this thought: "I am not practicing perfect insight." They do not form this thought: "I am both practicing and not practicing perfect insight." They do not form this thought: "I neither practice or do not practice perfect insight." It is by virtue of accord with these principles that bodhisattva-mahasattvas practicing perfect insight are said to be in accord with perfect insight.

COMMENTARY

Entertaining thoughts such as "I am practicing perfect insight" or "I am not practicing perfect insight" blocks penetrating insight by preoccupying the mind with self-consciousness. Classical Zen similes for insight emphasize this point by describing it as like "the eye that sees but does not see itself, the knife that cuts but does not cut itself."

3.

When bodhisattva-mahasattvas practice perfect insight, they do not see bodhisattva-mahasattvas, or perfect insight, or even these two names, either in the realm of the created or in the realm of the uncreated. Why? When bodhisattva-mahasattvas practice perfect insight they do not conceive notions of anything and have no alienated thinking. When bodhisattva-mahasattvas practice perfect insight they remain free from concepts.

COMMENTARY

The operation of insight is not the same type of mentation as formation of concepts, even religious or spiritual concepts. Although insight operates intuitively, on a different wavelength than reason, so to speak, that does not mean it is irrational; insight is neither reason nor unreason, neither rational nor alienated thinking. Zen texts often speak of those who misunderstand this point and become witless or deviated in the belief that they have "attained insight" by abandoning their reason.

4.

When bodhisattva-mahasattvas practice perfect insight, they should be realistically aware of the artificial definition of terms and the artificial definition of phenomena. Once they are realistically aware of the artificiality of terms and phenomena, they do not cling to matter, sensation, cognition, conditionings, or consciousness.

COMMENTARY

This passage follows on the preceding by illustrating the simultaneous use of both the rational and the intuitive modes of knowing. Realistic

awareness of artificial definiti
ventional truth; realistic awa
means insight into ultimate tr
are two sides of the same co
of relative and absolute truth.

When bodhisat
have no attach
the perfecti
tation, i
edge

All things have no existe
ment, the object of attach
the time of attachment are

COMMENTARY

This is not to be taken on faith as a doctrine but is to be examined
within oneself. Ungraspability is realized as an experience only after a
thorough mental search for the ultimate essence of something in itself.
This is a contemplative exercise, not a philosophical or intellectual
exercise. Some Zen preachers who cannot handle this type of material
have, nonetheless, often rationalized their avoidance of it, and their
eagerness to keep it from their disciples, by calling it philosophy. That
is a fundamental misunderstanding of the nature of Buddhist teaching
and is one way to tell a counterfeit roshi.

The point is illustrated in Zen tradition by a dialogue between the
Founder of Zen and his foremost disciple. The disciple said, "Please
pacify my mind for me." The Founder said, "Bring me your mind and I
will pacify it for you." The disciple said, "When I search for my mind,
I cannot find it." The Founder of Zen said, "I have pacified your mind
for you." At that the disciple awakened to the truth. To really understand this, one cannot jump by doctrinal declaration to the ungraspability of "I cannot find it" without having gone through the practice
of "When I search for my mind."

6.

...va-mahasattvas practice perfect insight, they
...ments to anything. Therefore they can enhance
...ons of charity, morality, tolerance, diligence, medi-
...sight, skill in means, commitment, power, and knowl-

COMMENTARY

Having no attachments to anything enhances charity in dissolving binding feelings such as personal pride or satisfaction at having given charity, a sense of reluctance or regret or loss or inconvenience or expense connected with giving, a feeling of superiority to the receiver, or a subtle sense of contempt for the receiver. By having no attachments to anything, perfect insight undermines the psychological complications and contaminations that come into play when self-interest, pride, and other fixations accompany the practice of charity.

Having no attachments to anything enhances morality because there is then no object of compulsion. Without attachment to anything, there is no mental obsession impelling one to act out—no greed to impel one to dishonesty, no hatred to impel one to aggression, no folly to impel one to imprudence. In classical Zen this was called the formless discipline of the mind ground; it is not based on rules per se but on transparent clarity of consciousness.

Having no attachments to anything enhances tolerance because there is then nothing at which to take offense, since one is not busy defending some conceptual, ideological, or egotistical territory against the imagined threats of differences and changes.

Having no attachments to anything enhances diligence because it saves mental energy otherwise expended on maintenance and constant renewal of a mental inventory and conceptual order taken for objective reality but demanding near total subjective involvement. Freed from the seeming solidity and worrisome weight of all that baggage, the insightful unattached mind saves and thus accumulates energy far greater than that which can be generated by ordinary motivational mechanisms such as desire or enthusiasm.

Having no attachment to anything enhances meditation by liberating the mind from the obstacles of its own making, such as circular thinking and emotionalized thinking. Restoration of original fluidity enables the meditator to freely enter and exit the broader ranges of human consciousness normally excluded by conventional mental habits. For meditators who habitually cultivate certain special states, having no attachment makes further progress possible, enabling them to avoid the sort of obsession known as "being reborn under the sway" of meditation states.

Having no attachment to anything enhances insight by liberating the mind from the distracting influence of internal suggestion, or what is called "the lull of words," which includes the persuasive power of conceptual thought, the mental storytelling process by which we describe to ourselves what we think of ourselves and the world as we suppose it to be. The stories we tell ourselves are ordinarily based on unexamined assumptions that precondition the way we understand ourselves and our stories; therefore nonattachment and insight have to work together to penetrate the hidden barriers of our inherited and acquired unconscious mental set.

Having no attachment enhances skill in means by disabusing the practitioner of any notion that there is only one way to accomplish the task of enlightenment. Insight without attachment enables us to utilize things without being ourselves used, or captivated, by things. This naturally includes religious forms. When observances are upheld after their usefulness has expired just because they have been inherited from earlier generations and have come to be thought sacrosanct, or when they are borrowed or imitated out of context by admirers without understanding who make them into cults, then the observances are not only futile in themselves, the obsessions of those who uphold them religiously interfere with, even prevent, the discovery or revelation and application of other means of accomplishing the same ends that the now defunct or situationally inapplicable observances were originally intended to achieve.

Having no attachment enhances commitment by enabling the individual to make objective choices without being prejudiced by personal predilections and to carry out altruistic undertakings without being influenced by hope for personal profit or reward.

Having no attachment enhances power by dissolving inhibitions and fears.

Having no attachment enhances knowledge by preventing the mind from making objects of knowledge into boundaries of consciousness and by undermining intellectual biases and conceits that limit receptivity to unknown knowledge.

7.

Subhuti said to Buddha, "World Honored One, since 'bodhisattva' and phenomena such as matter and so on cannot be grasped, to say that matter and other phenomena themselves are the bodhisattva-mahasattva, or that the bodhisattva-mahasattva is other than matter and so on; or to say that there exists a bodhisattva-mahasattva within matter and other phenomena, or that matter and other phenomena exist within the bodhisattva-mahasattva, or that the bodhisattva-mahasattva exists apart from matter—this is all incorrect."

Buddha said to Subhuti, "Good, good! So it is, so it is. It is as you say, Subhuti. Since matter and other phenomena are ungraspable, the bodhisattva-mahasattva cannot be grasped either. Because the bodhisattva-mahasattva, the great hero whose essence is enlightenment, cannot be grasped, the perfect insight practiced cannot be grasped either.

"Subhuti, when bodhisattva-mahasattvas practice perfect insight, they should learn in this way."

COMMENTARY

The seeker of enlightenment is not to be identified with the material and mental components of the human being, nor is the seeker to be imagined apart from those material and mental components. Identification produces a kind of self-consciousness that interferes with insight; dissociation causes debilitation of the faculties. Insight penetrates both barriers of identification and dissociation.

8.

Suppose good men and good women expound perfect insight for those who have set their hearts on supreme perfect enlightenment, or expound perfect meditation, or expound perfect diligence, or expound perfect tolerance, or expound perfect morality, or expound perfect charity, saying, "Come, and I will teach you to practice perfect insight, perfect meditation, perfect diligence, perfect tolerance, and perfect charity. Those who practice and learn according to my teaching will quickly realize the vehicle of hearers and the stage of individual enlightenment." These good men and good women are using formal descriptions as expedients, using possibilities of attainment as expedients, as well as the concept of divisions of time, to teach others to practice and learn perfect insight, meditation, diligence, tolerance, morality, and charity. This is in

actuality preaching imitation perfections of insight, meditation, diligence, tolerance, morality, and charity.

Suppose good men and good women expound perfect insight to those who have set their hearts on supreme perfect
enlightenment, or expound perfect meditation, or expound
perfect diligence, or expound perfect tolerance, or expound
perfect morality, or expound perfect charity, saying, "Come,
and I will teach you to practice and learn perfect insight, meditation, diligence, tolerance, morality, and charity. If you practice and learn according to my teaching, you will quickly enter
into the detachment that is the true nature of bodhisattvas.
Once you have entered into the detachment that is the true
nature of bodhisattvas, you will attain bodhisattvas' tolerance
of nonorigination. Once you have attained bodhisattvas' tolerance of nonorigination, you will attain bodhisattvas' nonregressive spiritual powers. Once you have attained bodhisattvas'
nonregressive spiritual powers, then you can traverse all the
buddha fields in the ten directions, going from one buddha
land to another supporting, revering, honoring, and praising
all the Realized Ones, the Worthies, the Truly Enlightened.
This way you will quickly attain supreme perfect enlightenment." These good men and good women are using formal
descriptions as expedients, using possibilities of attainment as
expedients, as well as the notion of points in time, to teach
others to practice and learn the perfections of insight, meditation, diligence, tolerance, morality, and charity. This is actually teaching imitation perfections of insight, meditation,
diligence, tolerance, morality, and charity.

COMMENTARY

The key point here is the limitation inherent in trying to teach transcendental perfections by means of formal descriptions, possibilities of
attainment, and notions of fixed points in time. The drawbacks to this
approach include the differences in understandings of formal descriptions, the tendency to confuse the imbibing of formal descriptions

with the acquisition of knowledge, the appeal of prospects of attainment to the greedy and aggressive elements of the worldly personality, and the shortcomings of a fixed sense or scale of time that cannot accommodate understanding of phenomena such as nonsequential events, retrograde motion, and differences in biological and psychological time. The perfections as preached in dogmatic or doctrinaire ways are called imitations because they are based not on the realities of life as it is but on the protocols of conceptualization and wishful thinking.

9.

Suppose good men and good women expound perfect insight to those who have set their hearts on supreme enlightenment, or expound perfect meditation, or expound perfect diligence, or expound perfect tolerance, or expound perfect morality, or expound perfect charity, saying, "Come, and I will teach you to practice and learn perfect insight, perfect meditation, perfect diligence, perfect tolerance, perfect morality, and perfect charity. While you are practicing and learning, do not view the principles as having anything to dwell on, to transcend, to penetrate, to attain, to realize, to accept and uphold, or any such virtues to be obtained or to rejoice in or to dedicate to enlightenment. Why? These perfections, from insight to charity, ultimately contain nothing to dwell on, to transcend, to attain, to realize, to accept and uphold, or any such virtues to be obtained or to rejoice in and to dedicate to enlightenment. Why? Because everything is inherently empty, having no existence. If they have no existence, then these are perfections, from insight to charity; in these perfections, from insight to charity, nothing at all can be grasped that has entry or exit, origination or destruction, annihilation or permanence, unity or variety, coming or going." If good men and good women explain in this way, this is expounding genuine perfections of insight, meditation, diligence, tolerance, morality, and charity.

Therefore good men and good women ought to use un-graspability as an expedient method for perfection of insight, remembering and reiterating it, thinking about it logically, they should use all sorts of skillful and subtle literary devices to expound it to others, setting forth and amplifying, clarifying and interpreting, analyzing meaning and import, facilitating their understanding.

COMMENTARY

The Zen classic *Blue Cliff Record* says that true Zen masters do not bind people with doctrines as if they were real things.

In an essay on perfect insight, Zen master Dogen writes that all the Buddhist teachings are "facilities of nothingness," echoing this scriptural instruction that practical teachings are not to be made into objects of attachment and obsession but are tools for a higher purpose.

10.

Shariputra said to Buddha, "Perfect insight neither augments nor diminishes all-knowledge."

Buddha said, "That is correct, because of ultimate purity."

Shariputra asked, "How is it that perfect insight neither augments nor diminishes all-knowledge?"

Buddha replied, "Because the realm of reality is permanent, perfect insight neither augments nor diminishes all-knowledge."

COMMENTARY

Perfect insight does not augment all-knowledge because it is not in itself an item or object of knowledge. Perfect insight does not diminish all-knowledge because it does not obliterate the characteristics of things.

Shariputra said, "Pure perfect insight has no fixations on anything."

Buddha said, "That is correct, because of ultimate purity."

Shariputra asked, "How is it that pure perfect insight has no fixation on anything?"

Buddha replied, "Because the realm of reality is immutable, therefore pure perfect insight has no fixation on anything."

———————————

The immutable realm of reality is all-pervasive, intuited by pure insight without fixing attention on differentiations of things.

11.

Shariputra said to Buddha, "World Honored One, because self is pure, all-knowledge is pure."

Buddha said, "That is so, because of ultimate purity."

Shariputra asked, "World Honored One, on what basis do you say that self is pure, so all-knowledge is pure, and this is ultimate purity?"

Buddha replied, "Self has no appearance, no attainment, no thought, and no knowledge, so all-knowledge has no appearance, no attainment, no thought, and no knowledge; this is ultimate purity."

———————————

The *Mahaparinirvana-sutra* identifies the real self with the buddha nature. Represented as the final teaching of Buddha, this scripture says the buddha nature is permanent, blissful, pure self.

12.

Shariputra said, "World Honored One, nonduality is pure and has no attainment and no view."

Buddha said, "That is correct, because of ultimate purity."

Shariputra asked, "On what basis do you say that the purity of nonduality, without attainment or view, is ultimate purity?"

Buddha replied, "There is neither defilement nor purification, so it is ultimately pure."

COMMENTARY

The nonduality of the absolute and the relative, summarized in the ultimate emptiness of all conditional things, means that the feelings and concepts of defilement and purity with which we view things are projected upon them by the views and assumptions of our own conditioned minds, in accord with our cultural and family backgrounds and our acquired patterns of habitual reactions to accumulated experience.

A general example of this principle is reflected in a proverb cited earlier, that for someone who is emotionally obsessed with Buddhism, in reality Buddhist teachings are in effect worldly things; whereas for someone who is not emotionally obsessed with worldly things, the things of the world are in effect enlightening teachings. Which is pure, which is defiled? Neither Buddhism nor the world is pure or defiled in itself; it is the way in which we think of them and treat them that creates the notions of purity and defilement as they are experienced and defined relative to one another.

13.

Buddha said, "Knowledge of the characteristics of the Way is realized on the basis of ultimate emptiness, boundless emptiness."

Subhuti said, "World Honored One, if bodhisattva-mahasattvas practice perfect insight, they do not remain on this shore, nor do they remain on the other shore, nor do they remain in midstream. This is how the perfect insight of bodhisattva-mahasattvas is ultimately pure."

Buddha said, "Knowledge of the characteristics of the Way

is realized on the basis of the equality of the nature of things of past, present, and future."

Not remaining on this shore means that the mind does not stick to things. Not remaining on the other shore means the mind does not stay in quiescent nirvana. Not remaining in midstream means the mind is not captivated by the process itself.

———————

The equality of the nature of things of past, present, and future refers to their relativity and emptiness of absoluteness. This implies malleability on the relative plane of conditional existence, which includes the possibilities of both construction and deconstruction, both concrete and abstract. It is on the basis of realizing this nature that one transcends the world ("this shore") to reach nirvana ("the other shore"); and it is also on this basis that one transcends nirvana to reenter the world deliberately.

———————

If one inwardly believed that time goes in only one direction and that things are inherently existing entities in fixed frames of time, then one would be subconsciously afraid to temporarily let go of the world mentally even if one had the idea that it could be done for a beneficial purpose. This psychological phenomenon is mentioned in the sutras on perfect wisdom, and in the recorded sayings of ancient Zen masters, who called it fear of falling into a void or abyss. Perfect insight opens the way to real liberation by penetrating this hidden barrier in full awareness.

14.

Subhuti said to Buddha, "World Honored One, if good men and good women on the vehicle of bodhisattvahood have no

skill in expedient means, they conceive mental images of perfect insight. Because they use the possibility of attainment as a
means, they abandon the most profound perfect insight and
become alienated from it."

Buddha said, "Bravo, bravo! So it is, so it is! It is as you say.
Those good men and good women relate to this perfect insight
by fixation on labels and definitions; they thereby throw it
away and become distanced from it."

Subhuti asked, "How do those good men and good women
get fixated on labels and definitions of this perfect insight?"

Buddha replied, "Those good men and good women grasp
labels and definitions of this perfect insight. Once they grasp
labels and definitions, they become obsessed with "perfect insight" and cannot actually experience insight into reality.
Therefore their type abandons the most profound perfect insight and becomes alienated from it."

COMMENTARY

This is one of the more explicit tests of insight. Some of the highly
abbreviated insight texts use arcane formulas like X is not X, or there
is no X in X, and as a result have been thought paradoxical. This
present illustration of alienation from real spirituality by fixations of
image and idea could be one of the most useful lessons of the insight
teachings for those who prefer realities to formalities.

15.

Buddha said, "If good men and good women on the vehicle
of bodhisattvahood have no skill in means, they grasp labels
and grasp definitions of this perfect insight; once they grasp
labels and definitions, they presume to have perfect insight
and become conceited, so they are unable to actually experience insight into reality. In this way, that type distances themselves from the most profound perfect insight."

When some of the Zen masters of old deemphasized the doctrines of Buddhism, they did so in environments where these doctrines were already known but were conventionally used in trade, as it were, for positions, offices, honors, and powers. Later followers who imitated them in their deemphasis of learning without having the knowledge to begin with degenerated in their meditations too because they lacked the guidance of the scriptures. Conceit on account of learning and conceit on account of ignorance are both conceit; that is what causes alienation from insight.

16.

Buddha said, "If good men and good women on the vehicle of bodhisattvahood have skill in means, they use ungraspability as means; they do not grasp at labels or definitions of this perfect insight and do not become obsessed and do not become conceited. Thus they are able to actually experience insight into reality."

"They use ungraspability as means" emphasizes the key point that this is not a doctrine or theory but a means, what is called in Zen a *shinjutsu,* or mental technique. This is often remembered by means of the story of the Zen Founder cited earlier, with the operative phrase "When I search for my mind, I cannot find it."

Scripture on Perfect Insight

THE QUESTIONS OF SUVIKRANTAVIKRAMIN

1.

Perfect insight is not susceptible to verbalization in terms of any principle or phenomenon. Perfect insight is beyond all verbal expression. Of perfect insight it cannot be said, "Perfect insight is by means of that," or "Perfect insight is from that." Even insight is not obtained or acquired, so how could perfect insight be acquired? Insight has no knowledge of all phenomena and has no recognition of all phenomena; therefore it is called insight.

How has insight no recognition of all things? All things are spoken of in one way or another, but all things are not apart from verbal expression. What has no knowledge or recognition of all things, words cannot express, except as people understand, by which it is called insight. This is called representation, so it is called insight.

COMMENTARY

The *Scripture on Unlocking the Mysteries* says, "Sages, with their knowledge and vision, detach from names and words and therefore actualize enlightenment." Detaching from names and words does not mean ignoring them or not understanding them but seeing through them, understanding that verbal descriptions are representations, not the essence of things in themselves. The ability to detach from words implies the ability to detach from verbalized mental processes, or mental processes using interior verbalization, here referred to as "knowledge" and "recognition" in their conventional senses.

2.

Things are not susceptible to representation, to establishment, to expression, to vision. Being without recognition is called having no recognition. Insight is neither without knowledge nor not without knowledge, nor is it unknowing knowledge; thus it is called insight.

COMMENTARY

Things are not susceptible to representation, establishment, expression, or vision, in that all of these operations are based on sense data and perceptual and conceptual organization and interpretation of that data. Objectively speaking, the "data," insofar as we are aware of it, consists of events within our nervous systems and is not the very same thing as what we mentally take it to represent. This is what is meant by the Zen saying that senses and objects fundamentally do not make contact with each other. When scripture says that insight is not recognition or knowledge, therefore, that means insight is not conceptual recognition of interpretations of sense data as if that were knowledge of objects thus represented.

3.

This is not the sphere of knowledge, nor of ignorance; it is not an object of ignorance or of knowledge. For knowledge has no object; if there were an object of ignorance, it would be ignorance. There is no knowledge from ignorance and no ignorance from knowledge; nor is knowledge ignorance or ignorance knowledge.

COMMENTARY

Neither knowledge nor ignorance means one is not clamping down on things mentally or telling oneself that water is wet, yet neither is one ignoring things or telling oneself that fire is cold. This is also described as having no conceptual notions of anything and having no alienated thinking.

Knowledge has no object insofar as its raw material is sense data, not the object itself as represented by the way the mind construes that data.

If an object of ignorance were known, that would not be ignorance but knowledge. Ignorance and knowledge, in their most thoroughgoing senses, do not produce one another in that they cannot coexist.

Knowledge is not so called on account of ignorance, nor is it called knowledge on account of knowledge. Knowledge is so called in reference to ignorance, but there is no ignorance in it of which it can be shown, "This is that knowledge, that knowledge pertains to this, that knowledge is by this means." Thus that knowledge is not there as knowledge, nor does that knowledge exist as an entity; the knowledgeness of that knowledge thereby is not found, nor is that knowledge founded on somethingness. Nor is ignorance referred to as knowledge.

Knowledge is not called knowledge in reference to anything of which it may be ignorant, yet it is not called knowledge because of a particular content. In another sense, knowledge is called knowledge in contrast to ignorance, yet any ignorance in reference to which knowledge would be defined cannot be found in knowledge itself.

Since this kind of knowledge is not there as knowledge per se, or as an entity or thing, it is therefore not of a kind with conventional knowledge understood as a body of learning, such as academic knowledge. The fact that this knowledge is not there as knowledge or as an entity means that no one can be possessive about it, attribute it to oneself, or take pride in it.

4.

If ignorance were called knowledge, then all ignorant creatures would be knowers. But perfect awareness of knowledge and ignorance as they are, without grasping either knowledge or ignorance—*that* is called knowledge.

COMMENTARY

Speaking on the relative plane, Confucius put this in ordinary terms when he told a disciple, "Shall I teach you how to know something? Realize you know it when you know it, and realize you don't know it when you don't." (*The Essential Confucius*)

Yet that knowledge is not as spoken of. Why? Knowledge cannot be verbalized, nor is knowledge an object to anyone, for knowledge transcends all objects. Nor is knowledge an object—this is exposition of knowledge.

In Buddhist terms, the knowledge that is nongrasping perfect awareness of knowledge and ignorance as they are is not one of the items of conventional knowledge but an all-pervading insight that is not subsumed or defined by any category of sense experience or intellectual knowledge.

5.

Clear understanding that is directly realized by intuitive perception is called transmundane insight; yet it is not transmundane insight as spoken of. Why? Even the world is not apprehended, much less insight beyond the world. How then could there be anyone who transcends the world by means of transmundane insight?

Why? It does not apprehend the world, so it does not cause transcendence of anything; thus it is called transcendent insight.

As for "the world," this is called a representation, and a representation is not beyond the world. What is totally beyond all representation is called transmundane.

The transmundane, furthermore, is not salvational; the transmundane is nonsalvational. Why? Nothing at all is found therein to be saved, or whereby to be saved—that is why it is called transmundane. For the mundane cannot be found in the transmundane, nor can the transmundane—the supreme of the supreme, it is therefore called transmundane.

This is called exposition of transmundane insight, yet it is not "transmundane insight" as spoken of. Why? Because what is transmundane cannot be verbalized; it is transcendental. There is nothing more in there to transcend—so it is called transmundane insight.

COMMENTARY

The mantra of perfect insight is "Gone, gone, gone beyond, totally gone beyond—enlightenment!" This is an encapsulation of the teaching presented here on transmundane insight, earlier encapsulated as "not remaining on this shore, not remaining on the other shore, not remaining in midstream."

6.

How can penetrating insight be penetrated?

There is nothing in it to be penetrated. Were there any-

thing to be penetrated, it would be represented as "insight penetrates." There is no penetration by anything, nor is there a
transcendence of anything that could be penetrated. In "penetrates" nothing penetrates, and there is nothing penetrated;
hence it is "penetrating."

There is nothing in it that reaches the end, or the middle
or meanwhile—hence it is "penetrating."

The penetrating penetrating is called insight. It penetrates
without running toward anything, going through anything, or
arriving at anything; thus it is called penetrating.

What does penetrating insight penetrate?

It penetrates any and every experience.

How does it penetrate?

It penetrates by insight.

What does it mean to penetrate by insight?

It penetrates [experiences] as representational definition.

Whatever is representational definition is indefinite.

Whoever penetrates with the insight that "representational
definition is indefinite" penetrates the mundane.

COMMENTARY

When we realize that the way we are experiencing things is mixed up
with our own interpretations of things and our reactions to our own
interpretations, we learn to refrain from taking our own representations for ineluctable realities, and thus reduce our susceptibility to
compulsion and obsession. Within the calmness and stability this insight produces, we can distinguish between subjective projections and
objective truths.

7.

How does one penetrate?

One realizes the mundane is immaterial. One does not penetrate any element herein, so one realizes the mundane is im-

material. One by whom the mundane has been penetrated is said to be imbued with penetrating insight.

COMMENTARY

Realizing the mundane is immaterial does not mean one can walk through walls, even though images like this are indeed occasionally used as metaphors for this insight. The mundane is immaterial because "the world" as we "know" it is a representation. Our minds hold on to this representation so firmly that it seems solid and real; that is what makes it "mundane." Learning to let go of representation is a way to direct witness of *suchness*, the objective reality for which there is no description. This letting go does not mean wrecking representation, for the faculty of representation is a useful and necessary tool for negotiating our way through infinity. After leaving the world, the Buddhist comes back, not dwelling either on this shore or on the farther shore. Damaging or destroying our power of representation in the name of detaching from it would debilitate us on the way; we would then drown in midstream, so to speak. Destructive deconstruction is not really detachment because it presupposes too much reality in representation to begin with; that is why it is said in Buddhism that deconstruction does not destroy anything. It is by understanding representation for what it is that detachment is attained, such that representation is not mistaken for absolute reality. Then representation is restored to its rightful place as a tool, instead of becoming a prison of the mind.

8.

How is one imbued with penetrating insight?

There is nothing bad to be penetrated; one realizes all is good, one transcends by penetrating insight.

One who penetrates everything he or she sees, hears, smells, tastes, feels, or cognizes is imbued with this penetrating insight.

How does one penetrate?

In terms of impermanence, painfulness, sickness, injuriousness, emptiness, hurtfulness, stressfulness, alienness, destructibility, inconstancy, perishability, selflessness, nonorigination, nondestruction, signlessness.

This is called having become cool, freed from pain.

Just as a type of medicine called *visalya* removes and destroys all stings wherever it is placed, so does a mendicant imbued with such truths, free from pain, cool, imbued with penetrating insight, abide at the ultimate end of routine existence, detached from everything mundane and gone beyond the noose of morbidity.

COMMENTARY

How can anything be at once empty and painful? If things do not really exist in themselves, how can they be called injurious? If all is good and there is nothing bad, how can anything be called hurtful? How are painfulness, injuriousness, or hurtfulness compatible with nonorigination or signlessness? The answer to these apparent paradoxes lies in distinguishing the particular nature of things under discussion—the imaginary or nonexistent nature, the relative nature, or the absolute nature. The painfulness, stress, and other negative attributes of everything refer to our conflicted experiences of things as we imagine them and react to them emotionally. The emptiness, nonorigination, and signlessness of things refers to their essential innocence of our subjective representations.

9.

Wherever a diamond is thrown to break something, it does break. Diamondlike concentration is like this: maintained by penetrating insight, wherever one applies it, wherever one operates it, everything is penetrated.

Being imbued with that penetrating insight, world-transcendent, reaching the true end of misery, is called unaffected triple knowledge.

Knowledge is a term for cessation of ignorance. Comprehension of ignorance means cessation of the mass of misery.

Suppose there is a physician who is learned, intelligent, skilled and reflective, versed in the use of all medicines, versed in the origins of all ailments, a reliever of all suffering. Whatever illness he treats, he relieves. Why? Because he is so well versed in the use of all medicines, well versed in the origins of all ailments, a reliever of all ailments.

Similarly is the third knowledge conducive to the cessation of all ignorance, the release from all misery, and the cessation of the whole mass of misery and depression from sorrow and lamentation over aging and dying. This is called world-transcending insight attaining penetration.

COMMENTARY

Triple knowledge refers to three kinds of all-knowledge. First is general all-knowledge, insight into the emptiness of all things. Second is knowledge of modes of the path, insight into the various ways in which enlightenment can be realized. Third is knowledge of all kinds, insight into the general and specific characteristics of things. These are also referred to as knowledge of emptiness, knowledge of the conditional, and knowledge of the middle way or path of central balance. The third knowledge is simultaneously aware of the absolute and relative.

10.

Supreme is the insight attaining penetration of the world, by which one accurately knows the end of becoming and birth.

What does "cessation of becoming and birth" refer to? It refers to penetration of origination and extinction.

How is origination and extinction penetrated?

Whatever is compounded all passes away—thus is origination and extinction penetrated.

Compounding means production, extinction means passing

away. Yet it is not origination and extinction as spoken of. Whatever is compounded is not an actual reality in itself.

Realizing that whatever is compounded inevitably passes away is understanding emptiness through impermanence. Realizing that a compounded thing is not an actual reality in itself is understanding essential emptiness. These insights are cultivated to foster detachment and liberate the mind from habitual fixations and compulsions.

11.

"Penetration" means understanding of interdependent occurrence. Whatever occurs that is dependent upon anything, being dependent on something else, it cannot be found to exist in itself. This is called penetration of interdependent occurrence.

That is understanding of interdependent occurrence as it really is, as unoriginated. For interdependent occurrence is unproduced; being the same as nonorigination, it is therefore called interdependent occurrence.

Where there is no production, how could there be destruction? Awareness of interdependent occurrence is extinction without destruction. Nonproduction is called interdependent occurrence.

What has no production has no origination; what has no origination is not past, future, or present; it cannot be found to have any destruction. That is called knowledge of nonproduction.

Whoever knows nonorigination creates no more, yet does not experience extinction. Whoever does not create does not destroy, knowing intuitively that the reality of origination is extinction. Whoever creates but recognizes, sees, understands, and realizes all things as extinct is thereby said to have experienced extinction.

COMMENTARY

The great master Nagarjuna wrote, "Interdependent occurrence *is* emptiness." He also wrote, "No thing can be found that has not occurred dependently; therefore no thing can be found that is not empty." He also wrote, "Samsara is none other than nirvana; nirvana is none other than samsara."

12.

Terminal knowledge means ignorance is terminated. Because ignorance is terminated, this is called terminal knowledge. How is it terminated? It is terminated in terms of interminability—no termination to it is seen. The cessation of ignorance is called terminal knowledge. Termination of ignorance is called terminal knowledge because it is perfect understanding of ignorance; yet ignorance is neither terminated nor not terminated, but its disappearance will be known, so that is called terminal knowledge.

COMMENTARY

Knowledge in this sense is not defined as a body of knowledge but as the termination of ignorance. That does not mean ignorance is posited as an objective state or object of intention and then terminated, but that the dissolution of ignorance is registered in awareness. Zen master Dogen wrote, "Just dig the pond, don't worry about the moon; when the pond is complete, the moon will naturally be there reflected in it." Digging the pond corresponds to the cessation of ignorance; the spontaneous reflection of the moon in the pond water when it is done represents the manifestation of knowledge.

13.

Understanding ignorance as it really is is called cessation. Nothing else is apprehended; this is called cessation of igno-

rance. Not even knowledge is apprehended, let alone ignorance; it is thus called terminal knowledge, but it is not as
spoken of. For anyone with terminal knowledge there is no
conventional usage, but this is expressed as termination of ignorance, or terminal knowledge.

COMMENTARY

While proposing liberation from psychological conflicts and afflictions, Buddhism cannot be considered escapist in any ordinary sense
of the word because it teaches cessation of ignorance by understanding it. This is the meaning of penetration.

14.

Whoever knows all things through examination of infinite
and finite knowledge goes beyond finite knowledge and
reaches the boundary of the infinite. The boundary of the infinite is the boundary of nirvana, yet it is not as spoken of.
Nirvana is inexpressible, apart from all conventional usage.

This is an expression of the realm of nirvana; yet it is not as
expressed, for the realm of nirvana is inexpressible, beyond all
expression. The realm of nirvana is apart from all expression.

COMMENTARY

Nagarjuna wrote, "Absolute truth cannot be expressed without resort-
ing to conventional usage; nirvana cannot be attained without coming
to absolute truth." He also wrote, "What is nonrelative and nongrasping is taught as nirvana."

15.

Perfect insight has no "this shore" or "the other shore." If any
near shore or other shore could be found in perfect insight,
the Buddha would teach the near or other shore of perfect

insight; but no near shore of perfect insight is to be found, so its "other shore" is not pointed out.

The distinction between "this shore" and "the other shore" is itself a view from "this shore," a barrier to penetration created by fixation on concepts and images.

16.

But perfect insight is the other shore of all things, of knowledge and works. That is why it is called perfect insight; and yet it is not as spoken of. For perfect insight is not arrived at by words or by acts; for perfect insight is inexpressible. It is recognition of all things, though recognition is contradictory. Why? There is nothing recognized here, nor penetrated, for enlightenment is equality of recognition and penetration; it is called enlightenment on account of recognition of all things.

Perfect insight is not arrived at by words or acts because it is not conceptual or intellectual knowledge such as might be conveyed by speech or writing, and there is no form of behavior whose conventional intentions or interpretations have any necessary connection to perfect insight. Two people may seem to be saying and doing the same things, but their perspectives and purposes may be quite different; one may be acting on independent insight, another may be acting on imitation of externals. One cannot know which is which without having insight oneself.

17.

How is enlightenment recognition of all things? There is no enlightenment herein, nor any recognition. Why? If enlighten-

ment were found, enlightenment would be found in enlightenment. But enlightenment is not to be found in enlightenment;
this is realized as enlightenment.

It is called recognition because of nonrecognition and non-
penetration, yet it is not as spoken of. For all things are unrec-
ognized and unpenetrated; nothing exists in and of itself. Thus
this is called enlightenment by virtue of this recognition.

Enlightenment is not obtained by the Buddha, nor is enlightenment represented by the Buddha. Enlightenment cannot be represented and cannot be taught. Enlightenment is not
ascertained or produced by the Buddha, for enlightenment is
not ascertained and not produced.

And enlightenment is not anyone's sphere, and there is no
being or representation of a being in enlightenment. Where
there is no being or representation of a being, how can it be
said, "This is an enlightening being" or "This is the perfect
insight of an enlightening being"?

COMMENTARY

Representation is not the same as reality; in that sense, things are un-
recognized and unpenetrated, for recognition and penetration are recognition and penetration of representation, not things in themselves.
Things do not exist in and of themselves, and so they cannot be
grasped; what we recognize are reflections of representations. Enlightenment by virtue of this recognition thus cannot be said to be a thing
in itself, even a state of mind or a domain of understanding, because it
penetrates all representations, even representations of enlightenment.

18.

There is no enlightenment in enlightenment and no being
in enlightenment. For this enlightenment is transcendent; this
enlightenment is unproduced; this enlightenment is unoriginated; this enlightenment has no external appearance. No
being is found or apprehended in it.

Enlightenment is not represented in terms of beingness, for recognition that there is no being is called enlightenment. Whoever knows enlightenment is beingless is called a bodhisattva or enlightening being.

Why? A bodhisattva is not revealed by the concept of a being; it is by virtue of not producing a concept of a being that one is called a bodhisattva. Yet it is not as spoken of. Why? A bodhisattva is inexpressible in words, for a bodhisattva is detached from the inherent essence of a being, for enlightenment is detached from all conceptions. Anyone to whom this enlightenment is known is called a bodhisattva.

Enlightenment is detached from all conceptions, including the conception of detachment.

19.

What does it mean that enlightenment is known? This enlightenment is transcendent, and this enlightenment cannot be fabricated, for this enlightenment is unoriginated and unperishing. Enlightenment does not represent enlightenment; indeed, enlightenment is not susceptible to representation. The unrepresentable, the incommunicable, the unproducible, is called enlightenment.

COMMENTARY

To say that enlightenment cannot be fabricated, represented, communicated, or produced means that it is not the maintaining of a particular system of beliefs or cultivation of a particular state of mind.

20.

One who perceives and cognizes without fanciful imagination, having divorced imagination, is therefore called a bodhisattva or enlightening being, but is not as spoken of. How so?

Because of beinglessness. If an enlightening being could be grasped, enlightenment would be obtained—"This is enlightenment, that is a being." But a bodhisattva is so called on account of recognition of beings as nonbeings and beingless. A bodhisattva or enlightening being is so called because of beinglessness, because of not developing the notion of being.

The realm of beings refers to nonbeingness, for no being is to be found in a being; it is the realm of beings on account of that not-being-found. If there were a being in a being, it would not be called the realm of beings. The manifestation of no realm is called the realm of beings, because the realm of beings is a nonrealm. If there were a realm of beings in the realm of beings, there would be the life and the body. Then there would be a realm apart from the realm of beings, because the realm of beings is realmless. "Realm" is a conventional expression, but there is no realm to be found in the realm of beings, nor is the realm of beings found in another realm of beings, for all things are realmless.

COMMENTARY

Perceiving and cognizing without fanciful imagination does not produce a sense of oneself as someone who is perceiving and cognizing, or a notion of perception and cognition, or a concept of having no fanciful imagination.

21.

No lack or fullness is found in the realm of beings. Why? Because of the beinglessness of the realm of beings, because of the disconnectedness of the realm of beings. Just as neither lack nor fullness is found in the realm of beings, so neither lack nor fullness is found in all things, for there is no absolute reality in all things in terms of which there could be lack or fullness. The recognition of all things as such is called recognition of all things.

COMMENTARY

The Third Grand Master of Zen wrote, "If you don't know the hidden truth, you work in vain at quieting thought. It is complete as space itself, without lack or excess. It is because of grasping and rejecting that you are not thus." (*Instant Zen*)

22.

Just as no lack or fullness is found in the realm of beings, so no lack or fullness is found in all things. The nonlack and nonfullness of all things, which is because of having no absolute reality, is itself the nonlack and nonfullness of the elements of buddhahood. Thus the nonlack and nonfullness of the elements of buddhahood is from recognition of all things. Because of the nonlack and nonfullness of all things, they are called elements of enlightenment.

Thus that refers to the elements of buddhahood, for the elements of buddhahood cannot be diminished or filled by anything. Why? It is recognition of all things, and in recognition of all things there is no lack or fullness of anything. "All things" refers to the elemental cosmos, and there is no lack or fullness in the elemental cosmos. Why? The elemental cosmos is infinite.

COMMENTARY

Things are said to have neither lack nor fullness on account of their emptiness of absolute reality because as such they have no intrinsic state of completeness in respect to which they can be lacking or full. In ordinary practical terms, seeing things as having no lack means acknowledging them as they are; seeing things as having no fullness means acknowledging change.

23.

No distinction can be grasped in the realm of beings and the realm of phenomena; nor can any lack or fullness be grasped or found in the realm of beings and the realm of phenomena. Realization of this is called enlightenment. So it is said that no lack or excess is perceived in the totality of the elements of buddhahood. "No lack and no excess" refers to seeing being as is without specific conceptualization. There is nothing to be removed or added to it. Realization of this is called enlightenment.

COMMENTARY

Seeing being as is without specific conceptualization, or alienated thinking, refers to the Zen experience of the mirroring awareness. This is practiced by taking everything in at once as a single total field of awareness without focusing on anything in particular or thinking about anything.

24.

Enlightenment is characteristic of Buddha. What is characteristic of Buddha? The outward appearances of all things are not intrinsic characteristics—this is the mark of buddhahood. For enlightenment has no appearance, being void of self-existence of appearances. Realization of this is called enlightenment, but not as spoken of. By virtue of realization of these truths one is called a bodhisattva, or enlightening being.

COMMENTARY

The pre-Zen author Sengzhao wrote, "The essence of sagehood is nameless and cannot be expressed in words; it is impossible to tarry in the empty door of truth as it really is."

25.

Anyone who considers himself a bodhisattva without knowing or realizing these truths is far from the stage of bodhisattvahood, far from the principles of bodhisattvahood. If one could be a bodhisattva by mere words alone, then all beings would be bodhisattvas. The stage of bodhisattvahood is not a mere word. Supreme perfect enlightenment cannot be realized by words. Enlightenment is not attained by speech, nor are the realities of bodhisattvahood.

COMMENTARY

This implies that intellectual, academic, or literary interests and activities in themselves are not of the essence of enlightenment.

26.

All beings carry out their activities within enlightenment but do not know or realize it, so they are not called enlightening beings. Why? Beings do not know the fact of nonbeing. If they knew, they would be bodhisattvas by virtue of their own actions.

COMMENTARY

According to the *Avatamsaka-sutra*, all people have the qualities and wisdom of buddhas latent within them but do not realize it because of false ideas and obsessive fixations. Knowing the fact of nonbeing here means understanding the unreality of false ideas and thus being liberated from the compulsive force of suggestion their repetition creates.

27.

Perverted beings, furthermore, do not know their own action, their own object, or their own sphere. If they knew their own action, they would not act on any false imagination anymore. By their actions based on false imagination all ignorant creatures act on unreal objects; they even think of enlightenment as an object. How can there be any enlightenment in those acts vis-à-vis objects, acts based on false imagination; how can these be qualities of bodhisattvahood? Those who know the truth no longer act on unreal objects and do not think of anything anymore.

A bodhisattva-mahasattva practicing perfect insight does not practice anything. Why? Because all things are established on the basis of unreality; they are nonexistent, false, not so.

COMMENTARY

People with inverted views project internal confusions and conflicts on external situations. They do not know their own mental habits, they do not realize they are objectifying their own thought processes, and they do not recognize the projections of their own ideas. If they knew how they themselves were distorting reality, they would see the source of their confusion and no longer be prone to act on erroneous assumptions, including assumptions about what enlightenment may be.

28.

As long as one practices anything, one is acting on unreality; acting on unreality, one does not act on reality. And bodhisattvahood is not manifested by acting on unreality, or manifested by acting on the nonexistent; a bodhisattva does not practice perfect insight acting on the unreal or the nonexistent. And what is unreal is nonexistent; there is no practice therein, so the bodhisattva does not act on it.

COMMENTARY

Zen master Baizhang said, "Now that you hear me say not to be attached to anything at all—good, bad, existent, nonexistent, whatever—you immediately take that to be falling into the void. You don't know that abandoning the root to pursue the branches is falling into the void. To seek buddhahood, to seek enlightenment, or anything at all, whether it may exist or not, is abandoning the root and pursuing the branches."

29.

"Unreality" means what is not so. This is grasped by ignorant creatures, not as it is. Those things that are not as they are taken to be are called unreal, hence nonexistent.

COMMENTARY

The *Avatamsaka-sutra* says, "Ignorant creatures produce sprouts of subsequent mundane life because of continually slipping into erroneous views, because of minds shrouded by the darkness of ignorance, because of being puffed up with pride, because of conceptions, because of mental fixations of desires caught in the net of craving, because of hopes pursued by actions in the tangle of deceit and falsehood, because of deeds connected with envy and jealousy producing mundane states, because of accumulation of actions rife with greed, hatred, and folly, because of the flames of mind ignited by anger and resentment, because of undertakings of actions bound up with delusion, because of seeds in the mind, intellect, and consciousness bound to the flows of craving, existence, and ignorance." (*The Flower Ornament Scripture*)

30.

So a bodhisattva-mahasattva does not act on the unreal or the nonexistent, the erroneous or the untrue. A bodhisattva is one who tells the truth and acts without falsehood. Where there is truth and reality, there is no practice; therefore the practice of the bodhisattva is said to be nonpractice.

COMMENTARY

There is no practice in truth and reality in the sense that one has already arrived, in the sense that truth and reality are not cultivated things, and in the sense that the evolution in the aftermath of this realization is spontaneous and involves no special effort.

31.

The practice of the bodhisattva is cut off from all practice. It cannot be indicated that "this is bodhisattva practice," or that "bodhisattva practice is by this means," or that "bodhisattva practice is herein," or that "bodhisattva practice comes from this." Bodhisattva practice is not manifested in this way.

COMMENTARY

When Qingyuan met the Sixth Grand Master of Zen, he asked, "What practice should one do to avoid getting stuck in stages?" The Grand Master said, "What have you done?" Qingyuan said, "I do not even practice the holy truths." The Grand Master said, "Then what stages are you talking about?"

32.

Bodhisattvas carry out bodhisattva practice by cessation of all practices: by cessation of the practices of ordinary people, by cessation of the practices of hearers, by cessation of the practices of individual illuminates. The bodhisattvas do not act on or devote themselves even to the elements of buddhahood with the ideas "These are the elements of buddhahood," "Here are the elements of buddhahood," "Hereby are the elements of buddhahood," or "The elements of buddhahood pertain to this." A bodhisattva does not act even in this way. All of this is acting on false imagination, or dissociated thought.

A bodhisattva does not act on thought or nonthought, for bodhisattva practice is void of all dissociated thought.

"Thought" is false imagining of all things. For things cannot be thought; all things are unthought, so whoever thinks of a thing is imagining falsely.

A phenomenon is neither a formal thought nor a dissociated imagination. "Formal thought" is one extreme, "dissociated imagination" is another extreme; and a bodhisattva does
not act on an extreme, nor yet on the unbounded.

One who acts neither on an extreme nor on the unbounded
does not observe the middle or mean. Acting on the mean
observing the mean is tantamount to acting on an extreme. For
the center has no practice, no seeing, and no showing.

COMMENTARY

The extremes being formal thought and dissociated imagination, acting on the unbounded is dwelling in abstraction or remaining in
thoughtless mirroring awareness. Zen master Baizhang explains that
even this is not to be made a point of fixation: "If you keep dwelling
in the immediate mirroring awareness, this too is tantamount to delusion." Zen master Hakuin wrote of this experience, "If practitioners
become fixated on the rank of the relative absolute, their cognition is
always affected by attraction and aversion, and their point of view is
biased." (Kensho)

The center has no *formally definitive* practice, seeing, or showing, because it is relative to extremes. One person's extremes of thought,
imagination, and emotion are not those of another, so there is no universal point at which to practice, perceive, or demonstrate balance.
Moderation for a glutton is not practiced or viewed in the same way
as moderation for a martinet; in either case it is moderation, but the
extremes being moderated are not the same, so the center of balance
is not the same.

33.

The center, middle, or mean refers to the noble eightfold
path. The noble eightfold path, however, is not established on
the basis of anything, nor by dint of observation of anything.

COMMENTARY

The noble eightfold path is said to have been a formulation used by Buddha to describe the way to the cessation of misery. The eightfold path consists of right seeing, right thinking, right speech, right action, right livelihood, right effort, right recollection, and right concentration. An interesting thing about this formulation is that the precise meaning of "right" is not generally defined; this is undoubtedly because the exact prescription would have to be based on individual conditions. This passage of scripture, in defining the noble eightfold path in terms of the center or middle way, skillfully provides a practical parameter without compromising the need to determine what is right for each individual according to circumstances.

It is apparent, from the texts on perfect insight, that there were those who had created intellectual and dogmatic edifices from the relics of Buddha's teaching. This is why one of the most famous texts on perfect insight says, "Buddhism is not Buddhism." In order to deter rigidly doctrinaire attitudes toward Buddhist teachings, the present scripture states that the noble eightfold path is not established on the basis of anything, or by dint of observation of anything. This means that the sufferings and the origins of suffering from which the eightfold path is designed to release people are not looked upon as ineluctable realities.

34.

When a bodhisattva does not construe or deconstruct anything, that is called the perfectly peaceful path. Neither construing nor deconstructing all things, having transcended cultivation, one realizes the equality of things, by virtue of which equality of things one does not even have the notion of a path, let alone see the path.

COMMENTARY

Construing things is the transmitted habit of naive realism, while deconstructing things by penetrating analysis is the cultivated practice of the elementary stage of Buddhism called the stage of hearers or listeners. The bodhisattva is one who has transcended the ingrained habit of construing things in conformity with conventional conditioning and already gone through the deconditioning process of deconstruction, whereby unconsciously imbibed misconceptions about the intrinsic identity and integrity of things and self are analyzed and unraveled.

35.

The "perfectly peaceful path" refers to sainthood entirely free from corruption. Why? That path is apart from what is caused to exist; it is neither caused to exist nor caused to nonexist. Therefore it is said to be apart from what is caused to exist. There is no manifestation in it, so it is said to be apart from what is caused to exist. Its manifestation is absent, so it is called nonmanifest.

COMMENTARY

The perfectly peaceful path is not a cultivated state, nor is it nothingness. It has no fixed form, nor is it something entirely amorphous. It is not attained by creating anything, or by destroying anything, or by revealing anything, or by concealing anything. It is not a particular set of actions, nor is it inaction per se. It is nonmanifest insofar as there is nothing concrete to point out as the perfectly peaceful path, or the beginning of the path, or the course of the path. That is what makes it perfectly peaceful.

36.

If there were any manifestation or disappearance, that would be apprehended, so it would not be unmanifest. "Nonmanifestation" means that its manifestation is absent, hence nonmanifest. It means its occurrence is absent, so it is called nonmanifesting, but it is not as spoken of.

Why? Because nonmanifestation has no articulation; absence is nonmanifestation. Absence in what sense? Not arising from error or unreality, not arising from the nonexistent or the untrue.

COMMENTARY

Those who brag about their modesty, show off their humility, take pleasure in privations, or otherwise pointedly pretend to practice what they preach—familiar impostors in all religions—illustrate the kind of "manifestation" that is "unmanifest" on the path of perfect peace.

37.

Unreality does not produce unreality; unreality has not occurred; there is no occurrence in it. As long as there is no occurrence in it, it should not be said that since it arises from what is nonexistent, hence it is called unreality, or error.

So a bodhisattva is aware of all things without unreality. Why? One knows unreality is nonexistent; there is no unreality to be found in unreality. Whoever knows unreality is nonexistent does not find unreality in unreality, so is aware of all things without unreality.

COMMENTARY

To be aware of all things without unreality means to see things directly without projecting false suppositions and arbitrary conceptions.

———————

Not finding unreality in unreality means knowing unreality for what it is, therefore having no illusions about what is unreal and not being distracted from direct insight by thoughts about the unreal.

38.

In realization of absence of unreality there is no more unreality; and when there is no unreality, there is no practice. For all practice is unreal because the performance of practice comes from false ideas of practice. But a bodhisattva does not falsely imagine practice, so all is said to be established without unreality. And whoever is alienated from reality practices something more; therefore bodhisattva practice is called nonpractice.

COMMENTARY

The word for unreality, or error, literally means "contrary to being." Since practices are set up to remedy errors, when the unreality of error is penetrated, there is no more "practice" to perform. Zen master Baizhang explains this in terms of the pragmatic order of incomplete and complete teaching: "To say that it is possible to attain buddhahood by cultivation, that there is practice and realization, that this mind is enlightened, that mind itself is buddha—this is Buddha's teaching, but these are expressions of incomplete teaching. . . . These are expressions concerned with weeding out impure things. . . . These are words for ordinary people. To say that one cannot attain buddhahood by cultivation, that there is no cultivation or realization, that it is neither mind nor buddha—this is also Buddha's teaching, but these are expressions of the complete teaching. . . . These are words beyond the teachings of the Three Vehicles, words of negative instruction, words concerned with weeding out pure things. These are words for someone of rank on the Way."

39.

"Nonpractice," or nonperformance, means that one does not act on any doctrine or practice any doctrine, or show any outward sign of practice; this is called bodhisattva practice. Whoever acts this way is acting on perfect insight.

COMMENTARY

Ancient Zen writings speak of carrying on "subliminal practice and inner application" while outwardly appearing unsophisticated and inconspicuous. A Chinese Zen proverb on this subject says, "A good merchant conceals his goods and pretends to have nothing." A Japanese Zen proverb says, "Miso that stinks of miso is not real miso."

40.

A bodhisattva is not acting on perfect insight when acting on the basis of material form; one is not acting on perfect insight when acting on the basis of sensation, cognition, conditionings, or consciousness. Why? All objects are known by the bodhisattva to be inaccessible; and there is no acting on what is inaccessible. Therefore bodhisattva practice is called nonpractice.

COMMENTARY

Objects are inaccessible in their essence, because we can only interpret sense data and cannot grasp objects in themselves. Insight does not act on assumptions, on conceptions, or on compulsions, realizing that these are projections of the subjective mind affording no means of access to objective reality.

41.

A bodhisattva is not practicing perfect insight while treating the eye as object. One is not practicing perfect insight while treating the ear, nose, tongue, body, or mind as object. Why? All objects are known to the bodhisattva to be nonexistent. And whoever knows all objects to be nonexistent does not act on them. Therefore the practice of the bodhisattva is said to be inaction.

COMMENTARY

On the level of naive realism, treating the eye, ear, and so on as objects may mean stimulating them compulsively; on the "listener" or "hearer" level of elementary Buddhism, treating these organs as objects means analyzing them. The exercise of perfect insight is already beyond the former habit and the latter practice.

42.

A bodhisattva is not practicing perfect insight when treating or acting on form, sound, scent, flavor, texture, or phenomena as object. Why? All objects are known to the bodhisattva to have arisen from unreality. And whoever knows unreality is nonexistent does not act on any object; therefore bodhisattva practice is called nonpractice.

COMMENTARY

Here again, treating or acting on form, sound, and so on as objects means fixation of attention on sense experiences. In the infantile stage of naïve realism, this fixation takes the form of cravings and repulsions; in the listening and hearing stage of elementary Buddhism, this fixation takes the form of analysis. When perfect insight is exercised, the fixation of attention itself is dissolved, so that the sense faculties can operate normally without the intellectual faculty's deceiving itself by its interpretations of their data.

43.

A bodhisattva does not practice perfect insight acting on name and form as objects. Why? All objects are understood by the bodhisattva to be baseless, nonobjective, so bodhisattva practice is called nonaction.

COMMENTARY

Name and form are the labels and descriptions conventionally assigned to normalized mental images of things and projected upon the world at large. Since these mental images, and their associated names and forms, can be manipulated so as to manipulate those who hold them, they are not taken for realities by those with liberated minds. A simple example familiar to everyone is the fact that a movement or an organization may be called a religion in name and have a formal liturgy and a concrete church, but that does not mean it is necessarily spiritual in nature. This is why there is really no paradox in the historical reality of the violence and oppression that have been carried out under the auspices of religions claiming goodness. There is no reason to assume that name and form correspond to reality. When this is nevertheless unconsciously assumed, that is because of a certain type of habit, not because of common sense or rational thought.

44.

Bodhisattva-mahasattvas do not practice perfect insight dealing with beings or self as objects. Why? The notion of being and the notion of self are known to them to be untrue, and whoever knows the ideas of being and self to be untrue does not act on anything. Therefore bodhisattva practice is called nonaction.

Those who do not act on anything have departed from performance, so bodhisattva practice is called nonperformance.

COMMENTARY

When the mind is fixed on self or others as objects, perception and awareness are formulated by the images of self and others being held in mind, while the energy of mind is continually expended in the maintenance of mental grasp on the imagery and its associated thoughts and feelings. The exercise of perfect insight, based on certain knowledge already realized, escapes these limitations by not holding on to these images, thoughts, and feelings, and not acting out under their compulsion. Being based on certain knowledge, this "letting go" is not associated with anxiety, regret, or other forms of residual attachment but restores the natural fluidity, buoyancy, and transparency of the mind to uncover its "buddha nature."

45.

A bodhisattva does not practice perfect insight while entertaining the notions of life, growth, person, personality, human being, youth, animator, instigator, creator, causer, data, perceiver, knower, or information. Why? All notions have been overcome by the bodhisattva, and whoever has overcome all notions no longer acts on any notions. In that sense it is said that bodhisattva practice is inaction.

COMMENTARY

The various notions enumerated here are elaborations and specifications of self-consciousness. Immersion in these ways of defining oneself and one's life experience solidifies a rigid sense of identity and a self-centered relationship to the world. This rigidity and bias not only impede direct witness of true reality but also prejudice the pursuit of ordinary aims as well.

———————

In the domain of formal religion, the notions of life, growth, person, personality, and so on are characteristic of careerism and conceit masquerading as piety and spirituality. Zen master Muso said, "Even after Buddha's death, all those who practiced the teaching appropriately gained some benefit. This was because they followed Buddhism only for liberation and for the salvation of all beings, not for social status and material profit. In later times, many people, both laity and clergy, followed and studied Buddhism for the sake of reputation and material profit. Therefore they did not advance in actual self-cultivation and refinement. They thought it was enough to learn the doctrines of the various schools. As a result, the more learned they were, the more conceited they became. In consequence of all this, whereas ordinary people have just the usual personal ego, students of Buddhism added to that a religious ego." (*Dream Conversations*) This also applies to other fields of endeavor, where competitive careerism and opportunistic self-seeking can compromise the quality, and indeed the very authenticity, of the work that is produced by professionals.

46.

Bodhisattvas do not practice perfect insight acting on unrealities, or on opinionated views, or on obstacles. Nor do they practice perfect insight dealing with unrealities, views, or obstacles as objects. Why? The objectifications of unrealities, opinions, and obstacles are thoroughly known to them; and perfect knowledge is not a performance, so in that sense it is said that bodhisattva practice is nonperformance.

COMMENTARY

Unrealities are errors of assumption, opinionated views are errors of interpretation, and obstacles are complications of emotion and intellect that interfere with clear objective awareness. Thorough knowledge of these phenomena implies thorough self-examination and discernment of the distorted actions and distorting effects of assumptions, opinions, and other psychological baggage. With thorough knowledge, it is realized that objectifying and acting on unrealities, opinionated views, or obstacles, whether in unconscious obedience to or deliberate defiance of their compulsions, imbues them with a sense of solidity and reality that they do not have in themselves when they are not energized by fixation of attention and acted out under the mesmerizing influence of preoccupation.

47.

Bodhisattvas do not practice perfect insight acting on the basis of interdependent occurrence. Why? Interdependent occurrence is thoroughly known to them; the basis of interdependent occurrence is thoroughly known to them. In perfect knowledge of interdependent occurrence and the basis of interdependent occurrence, there is no performance. Therefore bodhisattva practice is said to be nonperformance.

COMMENTARY

Acting on the basis of interdependent occurrence implies acting on an object to produce a cause. By its nature, as a mode of awareness, perfect insight does not act out anything or cause anything or produce anything. Perfect insight "penetrates" everything without destroying or changing anything objective. It might be said to undermine fixations of view and thought, but this happens through realization of the nonobjectivity of views and thoughts. Thus insight does not "do" anything and is itself nothing that can be performed as an act might be performed. Cultural habits of associating wisdom with particular performances, such as religious ritualism, academic intellectualism, political power, or commercial cunning, are therefore all in the domain of worldly convention and by their very formulation are radically dissociated from perfect insight in the Buddhist sense of the term.

48.

Bodhisattvas do not practice perfect insight acting on the basis of objectification of the realm of desire. Nor do they practice perfect insight acting on the basis of objectification of the realm of form or formlessness. Why? Because the objectifications of the realms of desire, form, and formlessness have been deconstructed, and there is no action in the deconstruction of objectification of the realms of desire, form, and formlessness, so it is said that bodhisattva practice is nonpractice.

COMMENTARY

The realm of desire is the ordinary world of passions and cravings. The realm of form is a range of consciousness in which forms are perceived without desire. Many meditation practices are carried out in this realm. The realm of formlessness is a range of consciousness in which there is neither desire nor form, only a succession of abstract experiences—infinity of space, infinity of consciousness, infinity of nothingness, and neither perception nor nonperception. Bodhisattvas have already been through these ranges of consciousness, have penetrated their relativity, and have deconstructed them in the sense that they know these are not absolute objective realities, and therefore they do not become fixated on them or obsessed with them, even on the level of experience, let alone description. This deconstruction does not "do" anything, since it does not literally dismantle anything, mentally or otherwise, but simply drops assumptions and illusions. Thus it is not a practice itself, but nonpractice of unnecessary mental habits.

49.

Bodhisattvas do not practice perfect insight acting on objectifications of generosity or envy, morality or immorality. Why? Objectifications of generosity, envy, morality, and immorality are thoroughly known to them. In thorough knowledge of objectifications of generosity, envy, morality, and immorality there is no action, so it is said that bodhisattva practice is nonpractice.

COMMENTARY

Ideological images of virtues and vices based on outward appearances may mislead people into misconstruing realities. As an earlier text illustrated, someone who appears to be generous may be acting in an outwardly charitable manner in pursuit of selfish ends. Someone may be called envious when merely voicing a legitimate complaint or criticism against those in positions of affluence and power. Those with public images as aggressive moralists may have adopted a posture of pompous piety to cover or distract attention from private indulgences; those who are benevolent to some people may be vicious to others. Unconventional and eccentric people may be branded mad or immoral, while those whom a society considers men of morality may have been called to account for their deeds only to the borders of their own communities or countries. In seeing what all these terms may possibly mean, including all the potential contradictions between name and reality, perfect insight does not require training in moral beliefs and cultivation of stereotyped virtues, because it sees things just as they are. No effort is required to take to the good and shun the bad because there is no confusion about what is good and bad. This can never be done just by rules—history amply proves this aspect of Buddhist teaching—so objectifications or fixed definitions of virtues and vices cannot be a basis for enlightened action.

50.

Bodhisattvas do not practice perfect insight acting on objectification of tolerance, intolerance, diligence, laziness, meditation, distraction, wisdom, or folly. Why? All objectifications are thoroughly known by them, and in thorough knowledge of all objectifications, there is no action. Therefore it is said that bodhisattva practice is nonpractice.

COMMENTARY

What appears to be tolerance may be forced acquiescence or feigned acceptance, either one concealing inward hatred or resentment. What appears to be intolerance may be unvarnished revelation of foresight into the eventual negative effects of currently accepted trends of thought and behavior of a given time. What may seem to be diligence may be a calculated show, a compulsion of some kind, or a waste of time on a whim or a wish. What may seem to be laziness may be disregard of trivialities. What may be thought to be meditation may be anesthesia, hypnosis, or fantasy. What may be thought to be distraction may be nonattachment to superficials, or ability to operate several departments of mental activity at the same time. What passes for wisdom may be platitudes and clichés. What people think is folly might simply be something they have never thought of before, or an action whose ultimate purpose they cannot perceive at once. Here again insight does not set out a fixed definition of virtues and vices and then proceed to try to put these notions into "practice."

51.

Bodhisattvas do not practice perfect insight acting on objectification of freedom from error, correct efforts, points of mindfulness, or the immeasurables. Why? All objectifications are known to them to be dependent, and thorough knowledge of the dependency of objectifications has no practice or action, so it is said that bodhisattva practice is nonpractice.

COMMENTARY

The correct efforts are elimination of negative mental factors that have already occurred, prevention of negative mental factors yet to occur, fostering positive mental factors as yet to arise, and enhancing positive mental factors already arisen. The points of mindfulness have already been mentioned. "The immeasurables" refers to boundless kindness, compassion, joy, and equanimity. These are all preliminary and preparatory practices designed to remedy character defects, dependent upon certain conditions for their specific necessity and for their actualization. Their pragmatic application in life experience is not the same thing as learning their definitions; celebrating them as religious principles, ideals, or goals in themselves; or publicizing personal presumptions of practicing or perfecting these exercises.

52.

Bodhisattvas do not practice perfect insight acting on objectifications of faculties, powers, branches of enlightenment, meditations, absorptions, or attainments. Why? Objectifications of faculties, powers, branches of enlightenment, meditations, absorptions, and attainments have been deconstructed by them; and there is no practice in deconstruction, so it is said that bodhisattva practice is nonpractice.

COMMENTARY

The faculties and powers referred to here are faith, energy, recollection, concentration, and discernment; these are called faculties when still latent potentials, powers when fully developed. The branches of enlightenment are discernment, energy, joy, comfort, recollection, concentration, and equanimity. The "meditations, absorptions, and at-tainments" refers to a system of four meditation stages and four form-less concentrations and attainments. The first stage of meditation is characterized by focused awareness, precise thought, joy, bliss, and single-mindedness. The second stage is characterized by inner purity, joy, bliss, and single-mindedness. The third stage is characterized by equanimity, mindfulness, precise knowledge, bliss, and single-minded-ness. The fourth stage is characterized by neither pain nor pleasure, equanimity, mindfulness, and single-mindedness. The four formless absorptions and attainments are absorption in infinity of space, absorp-tion in infinity of consciousness, absorption in infinity of nothingness, and absorption in neither perception nor nonperception.

———————

The word used in Buddhist Sanskrit for *deconstruct* means "make mani-fest" in Classical Sanskrit. Manifestation is implied in deconstruction in that what is deconstructed is what has been made manifest; were there no manifestation, what would be deconstructed? In pragmatic terms, this means that the bodhisattva has already cultivated the facul-ties, powers, branches of enlightenment, and so forth and then has deconstructed them, or deabsolutized and deobjectified them, by pen-etrating their relativity and letting go of mental images of them. Be-cause insight does not objectify, therefore the bodhisattva practicing perfect insight does not think, "These are the faculties and powers and so on," or "I have the faculties and powers and so on," or "I am practic-ing the faculties and powers and so on," or "I have realized the faculties and powers and so on." From the point of view of perfect insight, all of that mental activity is internal chatter, boasting, and presumption, not effortless insight.

53.

Bodhisattvas do not practice perfect insight acting on suffer-ing, its origin, its extinction, or the path to extinction. Why? Objectification of suffering, its origin, its extinction, and the path have been deconstructed by them. There is no cultivation in deconstruction, and no further performance, so it is said that the practice of bodhisattvas is nonpractice.

COMMENTARY

Suffering, its origin, its extinction, and the path to its extinction represent the teaching device of the four noble truths attributed to Buddha. This level of understanding the four noble truths is technically termed the unborn or birthless four truths. The great master of Tiantai Buddhism, whose meditation methods were largely based on perfect insight teachings, explains: "In the birthless four truths, there is no oppression in suffering; all is empty. How can there be emptiness that can get rid of emptiness? Matter itself is empty, and so are sensations, perceptions, conditioning, and consciousness; therefore there is no sign of oppression. The cause has no sign of combination; cause and effect are both empty. How can there be emptiness of cause and emptiness of effect combining? This applies to all desire, anger, and delusion. The Way has no duality; there is no one in emptiness, so how could there be two? Since things are originally not so, they do not now die out. Not so, no extinction; these are called the birthless four truths." (*Stopping and Seeing*)

54.

Bodhisattvas do not practice perfect insight acting on objectification of spiritual knowledge or liberation. Why? Objectification of spiritual knowledge and liberation is deconstructed by them, and there is no practice in deconstruction, so bodhisattva practice is said to be nonpractice.

COMMENTARY

Objectifications of spiritual knowledge and liberation are mental images or ideas of spiritual knowledge and liberation, not the experience of spiritual awareness and mental freedom.

55.

Bodhisattvas do not practice perfect insight acting on objectification of nonorigination, or objectification of extinction, or objectification of nonconstruction. Why? Objectification of nonorigination, extinction, and nonconstruction is deconstructed by them, and there is no further action in deconstruction, so bodhisattvas' practice is said to be nonpractice.

COMMENTARY

Nonorigination, extinction, and nonconstruction, all Buddhist technical terms, are considered most difficult to understand precisely because of the mental habit of objectification. Since nonorigination, extinction, and nonconstruction can be nothing in themselves but refer to the nonproduction of mental fixations, either wrestling with intellectual definitions or trying to cultivate absence of mind will only take one further away from the experience of what these terms really mean.

56.

Bodhisattvas do not practice perfect insight acting on objectification of water, fire, air, or space. Why? Objectification of water, fire, air, and space have been deconstructed by them, and in deconstruction there is no practice, so it is said that the practice of bodhisattvas is nonpractice.

COMMENTARY

Visualization of elements of water, fire, air, and space is an ancient practice designed to develop mental concentration and provide access to an impersonal view of existence. Indulged in for its own sake, this practice becomes a dead-end trap. Insight penetrates the relativity of the experiences this practice fosters, therefore undermining the basis of obsession.

57.

Bodhisattvas do not practice perfect insight acting on objectification of the states of listeners and individual illuminates. Why? Objectifications of the states of listeners and individual illuminates have been deconstructed by them, and there is no practice in deconstruction, so it is said that bodhisattva practice is nonpractice.

COMMENTARY

An ancient Zen master said, "The teaching has no fixed form; whatever you encounter is the source." Citing this, a later Zen master said, "The methods of teaching used by the wise to guide learners have no fixed form or appearance." (*Dream Conversations*)

58.

Bodhisattvas do not practice perfect insight treating nirvana as an object. Why? Nirvana as an object, or objectification of nirvana, is thoroughly known to them, and in thorough knowledge there is no practice, so it is said that bodhisattva practice is nonpractice.

COMMENTARY

The *Lotus Sutra* calls nirvana an illusory citadel, a temporary refuge for the weary of spirit who otherwise could not face the infinite eternity of the road of complete enlightenment. The *Sutra on Unlocking the Mysteries* refers to "quiescent nirvana" as "the highest expedient." The expediency of nirvana implies that it is not an objective but a means.

———————

Zen master Muso said, "It is axiomatic in all Mahayana Buddhist schools that there is no discrepancy between Buddhism and worldly phenomena; no genuine teacher could say there is practice of Buddhism outside of events and activities. Nonetheless, people who do not understand this entertain false ideas about things of the world, so Zen teachers expediently tell them to let go of things temporarily so as to enable them to get rid of their fixations." (Dream Conversations)

59.

Bodhisattvas do not practice perfect insight treating purification of attributes as an object, or treating purification of buddha lands as an object, or treating the attainment of listeners as an object, or treating attainment of bodhisattvahood as an object. Why? Because the object of purification of attributes, the object of purification of buddha lands, the object of the attainment of listeners, and the object of the attainment of bodhisattvas have been deconstructed by them. And there is no practice in deconstruction, so it is said that bodhisattva practice is nonpractice.

COMMENTARY

Perfect insight is sometimes called the fundamental ground in Zen, because it is central to liberation; purification of attributes, buddha lands, and spiritual ranks are commonly "deconstructed" in Zen sayings intended to illustrate the fundamental ground of penetrating insight. Zen master Muso explained, "The fundamental ground is a term provisionally applied to the point where illusion and enlightenment are undifferentiated, to which no worldly names or descriptions apply, and which even transmundane teachings do not reach." (Dream Conversations)

60.

Practicing thus do bodhisattvas practice perfect insight. This is the practice of bodhisattvas practicing perfect insight, the practice of thorough knowledge of all objects, the practice of deconstruction of all objects, so-called practice of perfect insight.

COMMENTARY

Muso said, "To reach the fundamental ground is not something like going from the country to the city, or from one land to another. In reality it is like waking up from a dream. All the questions about where the fundamental ground is and how to get there are part of the dream, arising from dreaming thoughts about a dream." (*Dream Conversations*)

61.

The bodhisattva practicing thus does not even deal with the purification of matter objectified, nor with the purification of objectification of sense, cognition, patterns of conditioning, or consciousness. Why? Matter objectified is thoroughly known by the bodhisattva to be perfectly pure by nature, and so are sense, cognition, conditioning, and consciousness thoroughly known to be so, by virtue of which knowledge this practice is the bodhisattva's practice of perfect insight.

Practicing thus, the bodhisattva does not deal with the purification of the eye objectified, nor with the purification of the ear, nose, tongue, body, or mind objectified. Why? Because it is all thoroughly known to the bodhisattva to be perfectly pure by nature, by virtue of which knowledge this practice is the bodhisattva's practice of perfect insight.

Practicing thus, the bodhisattva does not deal with even the purification of objectification of form, sound, scent, flavor, texture, and phenomenon. Why? Because it is all thoroughly known to the bodhisattva to be perfectly pure by nature, including objectification of phenomena, or phenomena as objects, which very practice is the bodhisattva's practice of perfect insight.

Practicing thus, the bodhisattva does not even deal with purification of objectifications of name and form. Why? Objectification of name and form is thoroughly known to the bodhisattva to be perfectly pure by nature, which very practice is the bodhisattva's practice of perfect insight.

Practicing thus, the bodhisattva does not even deal with purification of objectifications of self and being. Why? Objectification of self and being is thoroughly known to the bodhisattva to be perfectly pure by nature, which very practice is the bodhisattva's practice of perfect insight.

Practicing thus, the bodhisattva does not even deal with purification of objectifications of life, existence, personality, agency, instigation, animation, arousal, information, communication, or opinion. Why? Objectifications of life, existence, personality, agency, instigation, animation, arousal, information, communication, and opinion are known to the bodhisattva to be perfectly pure by nature, which very practice is the bodhisattva's practice of perfect insight.

Practicing thus, a bodhisattva does not even deal with purification of objectification of error and opinionation. Why? Objectification of error and opinionation is thoroughly known to the bodhisattva to be perfectly pure by nature.

Practicing thus, a bodhisattva does not even deal with purification of objectifications of interdependent occurrence; the realms of desire, form, and formlessness; generosity or envy, morality or immorality; tolerance or intolerance, diligence or laziness, meditation or distraction, wisdom or folly; past, future, or present; nonattachment; superknowledge; or omniscience.

Practicing thus, a bodhisattva practices perfect insight who does not deal with the purification of any objectification whatsoever. Why? Because of the natural perfect purity of all objects.

COMMENTARY

If we try to purify something, that means we have already reified it and judged it impure. This is needed at the infantile state where we need to learn not to eat paint chips, not to hurt our companions, and other matters of common sense. Subsequently different life contexts and stages of social development present different frameworks for perceiving relative purity and impurity. At the level of maturity where people are ready to practice perfect insight, purity has a different meaning from contrast to impurity. Natural perfect purity of all objects is a technical expression for emptiness, referring to the disconnection between objective reality in itself and subjective experiences construed as realities. In practical terms, this implies that things in themselves are neither good nor bad, neither pure nor impure, except in terms of our relationships with them and our uses of them. Zen masters say that it is good to be able to see what is bad about what we like and what is good about what we don't like. This is an example of a way of application of insight into natural purity by using concepts and judgments deliberately to look outside the boundaries of those concepts and judgments. Zen metaphor calls this the finger pointing at the moon— don't look at the finger, behold the moon.

62.

Practicing thus, a bodhisattva does not observe, "This is form," does not observe, "Form is hereby," does not observe, "Form belongs to this," does not observe, "Form comes from this." Nonobserving form in this way, one does not set up form or throw away form, nor produce or destroy form, nor ruminate on form, nor dissociate from form, nor deal with or dissociate from objectification of form. Practicing thus does a bodhisattva practice perfect insight.

In the same way, one does not observe, "These are sensation, cognition, conditionings; this is consciousness." One does not observe, "Consciousness is hereby," does not observe, "Consciousness belongs to this," does not observe, "Consciousness comes from this." Nonobserving consciousness in this way, one does not set up consciousness or throw away consciousness, nor produce consciousness nor destroy consciousness, nor act on consciousness nor dissociate from consciousness, nor act on or dissociate from objectification of consciousness. Thus does a bodhisattva practice perfect insight.

COMMENTARY

These are working definitions of the middle way of centered balance in respect to forms, sensations, cognitions, conditionings, and consciousness—neither setting up nor throwing away, neither producing nor destroying, neither ruminating nor dissociating. In this manner the mental attitude is neither obsessive nor evasive, neither affirmative nor negative.

63.

A bodhisattva practicing thus does not consider form to be past, does not consider form to be yet to come, does not consider form to be present. In the same way, a bodhisattva does not consider sensation, cognition, conditionings, or consciousness to be past, yet to come, or present.

COMMENTARY

What is past cannot be grasped because it is already gone. What is yet to come cannot be grasped because it has not occurred. What is present cannot be grasped because it is in flux.

64.

A bodhisattva does not consider form as self, does not consider form as belonging or pertaining to self. Likewise, one does not consider sensation, cognition, conditions, or consciousness to be self or to belong or pertain to self.

COMMENTARY

This is experiencing experience without identifying with it or being possessive about it.

65.

One does not consider form painful, nor does one consider sensation, cognition, conditionings, or consciousness to be painful.

COMMENTARY

Painfulness as we experience it is in the nature of our relationships with form, sensation, cognition, conditionings, and consciousness. To resolve the problem of existential painfulness requires attention to the quality of these relationships, not repetition of thoughts of these phenomena as painful.

66.

One does not consider form to be one's own or others'. One does not consider sensation, cognition, conditionings, or consciousness to be one's own or others'. Thus does a bodhisattva practice perfect insight.

COMMENTARY

None of these things could ultimately belong to us in view of the fact that we have to die, and this manner of contemplation may be used to detach from such thoughts.

If we think of experiences of some kind as our own and not common to others, or as characteristic of others and not of ourselves, this tends to cause conceit and curtail compassion.

67.

A bodhisattva practicing perfect insight does not deal with the origination of form or the destruction of form, does not consider form profound, does not consider form shallow, does not consider form empty, does not consider form nonempty, does not consider form to be appearance, does not consider form to be without appearance, does not consider form purposeful, does not consider form purposeless, does not consider form to be formation, does not consider form to be without formation.

In this way, one does not deal with the origination of sensation, cognition, conditionings, or consciousness, does not deal with destruction of consciousness, does not consider consciousness deep, does not consider consciousness shallow, does not consider consciousness empty, does not consider consciousness nonempty, does not consider consciousness to be appearance, does not consider consciousness to be without appearance, does not consider consciousness purposeful, does not consider consciousness purposeless, does not consider consciousness as being formed, does not consider consciousness as being unformed.

COMMENTARY

The practice of insight is not the same thing as creating certain forms or destroying all forms, or producing certain sensations, cognitions, conditionings, or states of consciousness, or obliterating these modes of experience.

Considering phenomena deep or shallow depends upon separate consideration of their metaphysical nature and concrete characteristics. In accordance with the middle way of centered balance, phenomena are neither taken too seriously nor ignored too studiously.

Phenomena are not empty in the sense that nothing exists at all, so insight does not consider them empty that way; yet phenomena are dependent and have no absolute existence in any event, so insight does not consider them nonempty in that sense.

Appearances are not absolute realities, yet they are not absolutely non-existent either.

Phenomena do not themselves have the purposes or aims for which we try to utilize them or which when hopelessly compelled or thwarted we project upon them, and yet the manifest laws of causality that govern their relative existence mean that phenomena cannot be effectively considered random and purposeless either.

Matter, sensation, cognition, conditionings, and consciousness cannot be considered formed because they are malleable, changeable, and have no permanent inalienable forms. Nevertheless, they cannot be effectively considered unformed because their specific manifestations and operations are not amorphous nothingness or undefined data.

68.

Why? All these are imagined, supposed, projected, falsified, fancied. "I consider" is projected; "Hence I proceed" is falsified; "I deal with this" is fancied; "Here I carry out practice" is imagined.

COMMENTARY

A Zen proverb says, "If you know what kind of dream it is, the dream will be awakened." When insight espies the hidden agendas of imagination, supposition, projection, falsification, and fancification, the spell they cast on the mind is broken.

69.

Knowing all these here to be imagined, projected, falsified, and fancied, bodhisattvas do not think of anything destructive to all-knowledge; not thinking, they do not practice anything or depend on anything. They are independent, neither attached nor detached; they do not set anything up, nor do they establish anything. This is the destruction of all thinking by the bodhisattva practicing perfect insight.

COMMENTARY

Some people mistake destruction of thinking for being thoughtless, or for keeping the mind frozen still as much as possible. These are objectifications of not thinking, not the real experience. The Sixth Grand Master of Zen explained, "When the mind is not influenced by objects, this is called freedom from thought. One is always detached from objects in one's own thoughts, and one does not arouse the mind over objects. If you just do not think of anything at all, and get rid of all thoughts entirely, once all thoughts end you die and come back to life someplace else. This is a big mistake; those who study the Way should think about it." (*The Sutra of Hui-neng, Grand Master of Zen*) "Coming back to life someplace else" after "dying" when thoughts end means that repressed mental habits and unconscious propensities eventually reassert themselves. That is why concentration without insight cannot effect liberation.

70.

Furthermore, the bodhisattva practicing perfect insight thus does not consider form permanent or impermanent, does not consider form empty or nonempty, does not consider form like illusion, does not consider form like a dream, does not consider form like a reflection, does not consider form like an echo; and so also sensation, cognition, conditioning, and consciousness. One does not consider consciousness permanent or impermanent, does not consider consciousness empty or nonempty, does not consider consciousness like an illusion, does not consider consciousness like a dream, does not consider

consciousness like a reflection, does not consider consciousness like an echo.

Why? These are all thought up, conjectures, falsely construed by customary practice. The bodhisattva, knowing these
are all thought up, conjectures, falsely construed by customary
practice, then practices perfect insight to remove all courses of
action, to thoroughly know all courses of action.

COMMENTARY

Zen master Muso says, "If people who are not yet in communion with
the inherent mind of enlightenment consider relentless devotion to
religious practice to be evidence of firmness of will for enlightenment
and power in practice, they will certainly become obsessed because of
their pride. Then again, there is also the anxiety that if this determina-
tion weakens and they are distracted by worldly conditions, then they
will not attain salvation. Thus inherent enlightenment becomes in-
creasingly obstructed and obscured by this pride and this fear." (Dream
Conversations)

71.

This bodhisattva practice of perfect insight is inconceivable
because of the inconceivability of form. In the same way, this
bodhisattva practice of perfect insight is inconceivable because
of the inconceivability of sensation, cognition, conditionings,
and consciousness.

This bodhisattva practice of perfect insight is inconceivable
because of the inconceivability of name and form; interdependent occurrence; affliction; fruition of actions; substance; unreality; opinionation; realms of desire, form, and formlessness;
self; being; generosity; stinginess; morality; immorality; tolerance; hostility; diligence; laziness; meditation; distraction; wisdom; folly; greed, hatred, and delusion; points of mindfulness;
right efforts, annulments of errors, and bases of spiritual powers; faculties, powers, and branches of enlightenment; concen-

tration; attainment; mundane courses of life; suffering, origin, extinction, and the path; knowledge and liberation; knowledge of extinction, knowledge of nonorigination, and knowledge of nonconstruction; stages of listeners, stages of individual illuminates; states of listeners and individual illuminates; super-knowledge; past, future, and present; unattached knowledge; nirvana; and buddhahood.

Why? A bodhisattva's practice of perfect insight does not produce thought; so it is said to be inconceivable.

COMMENTARY

Inconceivability implies inaccessibility to conceptualization. Perfect insight does not use conceptualization to understand anything.

The *Avatamsaka-sutra* says, "If people want to really know all buddhas of all times, they should contemplate the nature of the cosmos—all is but mental construction." It also says, "The grasped cannot be grasped, the seen cannot be seen, the heard cannot be heard; the one mind is inconceivable." (*The Flower Ornament Scripture*)

Because insight does not produce thought, some have imagined that suppressing thought is insight, or leads to insight. Zen master Mi-an said, "People temporarily halt sensing of objects, then take the bit of light that appears before their eyes to be the ultimate. This sickness is most miserable." (*Instant Zen*)

72.

Arousal of thought is unrealism. "Thought producing thought" is a contradiction in thinking, because the nature of thought itself does not arise and is not born. Thought arises in connection with unreality; there the thought is apparent, and the unreality or error by which it arises is also apparent.

COMMENTARY

Zen master Mazu said, "A single thought of the wandering mind is the root of birth and death in the world." To say that thought connected with unreality is apparent, and the unreality of the error on which it is based is apparent, implies that it is possible to witness this process without being carried away or deceived by it. That is how it is said that insight sees the true aspect of things without obliterating their appearances.

73.

Yet ignorant people do not know that the apparent is thought; and whenever it arises, that is the apparent, and however it arises, that is the apparent. Not knowing the disconnectedness of thought, not knowing the disconnectedness of objectification, they get totally into the notions "I am thinking," "my thought," "thought of this," and "thought deriving from this."

Having gotten totally into thought, they become fixated on the notions of good, bad; pleasant, painful; finite, infinite; opinion; interference; generosity and stinginess; morality and immorality; the realm of realities, the realm of desires, the realm of forms, the realm of formlessness; interdependent occurrence; name and form; greed, hatred, and delusion; envy and jealousy; egotism; suffering, its origin, its extinction, the path to extinction; and so on.

A bodhisattva, seeing people with such fixations, producing erroneous thoughts, does not give rise to any thought about error. Why? Perfect insight is apart from thought, and in the natural clarity and natural purity of thought there is no arousal of thought.

COMMENTARY

Zen master Mazu said, "Human delusions of time immemorial—deceit, pride, deviousness, conceit—are conglomerated into one body.

That is why scripture says that this body is just made of elements, and its appearance and disappearance is just that of elements, which have no identity. When successive thoughts do not await one another, and each thought dies out peacefully, this is called absorption in the oceanic reflection." (*Zen Essence*)

74.

Ignorant people produce thought in reference to the existence of an object. Thus a bodhisattva, while also discerning an object, discerns the arising of thought. Why does thought arise? A bodhisattva observes that this thought is naturally clear, so it occurs to the bodhisattva that the thought arises relative to the object. Thoroughly knowing the object, one does not produce thought, nor yet extinguish thought. That thought occurs to the bodhisattva as clear, unafflicted, pleasant, perfectly pure.

COMMENTARY

Natural clarity is an insight into the relativity-equals-emptiness equation, in which the characteristics of thoughts are evident but have no blinding opacity because insight can see right through their relativity and emptiness of objectivity. This penetration is effortless because it is realized without obliterating the appearances of thoughts or phenomena.

75.

The bodhisattva stabilized in the nonproduction of thought does not produce anything or destroy anything. This is the thorough knowledge of nonproduction of thought of the bodhisattva practicing perfect insight. It does not occur to one practicing thus, "I am practicing perfect insight," "Here I practice perfect insight," "Hereby I practice perfect insight," or "Hence I practice perfect insight." For if one conceives "This is perfect insight," or "Perfect insight is hereby," or "Perfect insight pertains to this," then one is not practicing perfect insight. So one does not even observe or grasp that perfect insight, or think, "I am practicing perfect insight," but actually applies perfect insight.

COMMENTARY

You can tell you're not applying insight when you think you are practicing it or when you think your thoughts are insights.

76.

This practice of the bodhisattva, that is the practice of perfect insight, is unexcelled, clear, unsurpassed, transcendent. It is inaccessible to morbidity, to factors of morbidity, to any who follow appearances, who follow attainment, who have views of self, who have views of being, who have views of life, who have views of personality, who have views of existence, who have views of nonexistence, who have views of nihilism, who have views of permanence, who have views of their own bodies, who have views of the clusters, who have views of the elements, who have views of the sense media, who have views of Buddha, who have views of Dharma, who have views of Sangha, who have views of nirvana, who have a sense of attainment, or who are conceited, or who act on greed, hatred, or folly, or who act on unreality, or who are on a wrong path. This practice of the bodhisattva, namely the practice of perfect insight, is the practice of rising above all worlds.

COMMENTARY

This passage is too eloquent for further comment.

77.

A bodhisattva practicing perfect insight penetrates the cause, origination, ending, and extinction of all things; there is nothing irrelevant to perfect insight. One knows the character of the cause, origin, extinction, and course of all things; yet while knowing the cause, origin, extinction, and course of all things, one does not cultivate or deconstruct form, or sensation, or cognition, or conditionings; one does not cultivate or deconstruct consciousness, or name and form; or affliction or purification; or error, opinionation, or obstructions; or greed, hatred, or folly; or the realms of desire, form, or formlessness; or the realm of beings or the realm of self; or the notion of annihilation or the notion of permanence; generosity or stinginess; morality or immorality; tolerance or intolerance; diligence or laziness; meditation or distraction; wisdom or ignorance; points of mindfulness, correct efforts, annulments of errors, or bases of spiritual powers; faculties, powers, branches of enlightenment, concentrations, or attainments; interdependent occurrence; malaise, its origin, its extinction, or the way; knowledge of nonorigination, knowledge of ending, knowledge of noncreation; the stage of ordinary people, the stage of learners, the stage of individual illuminates, the stage of enlightening beings; principles of ordinary people, principles of learners, principles of individual illuminates; stopping and seeing; nirvana; knowledge and vision of past, future, and present; attachment; nonattachment; buddha knowledge; buddhas' confidences.

Why? Because form, sensation, cognition, conditioning, and consciousness cannot be cultivated; name and form, unreality and opinionation, points of mindfulness, correct efforts, bases of spiritual powers, annulments of errors; the immeasurables; the faculties, powers, and branches of enlightenment; the absorptions, attainments, and superknowledges; the knowledge of ending; and the knowledge of noncreation cannot be cultivated or brought into existence.

The stage of ordinary people cannot be cultivated; the stages of listeners, individual illuminates, and enlightening beings cannot be cultivated. The principles of ordinary people, listeners, and individual illuminates cannot be cultivated.

Knowledge and vision of past, future, and present cannot be cultivated. Unattached knowledge and vision cannot be cultivated. Unfocused knowledge and vision cannot be cultivated. Perfectly enlightened knowledge cannot be cultivated.

Why? Because there is no ultimate completion to becoming; none of these conventions or usages is really existent; there is no intrinsic being in them.

For all things are void of intrinsic being, not having come to be, not actually existent.

Why? What is unreal is nonexistent, and all things are established on the basis of unreality.

Unreality has no becoming, and all things are void of becoming; becoming is not apprehended, because of the nonexistence of intrinsic being. What has no becoming has not come to be, so it does not actually exist.

COMMENTARY

Nothing is irrelevant to insight in that it applies to everything. The observation that there is no ultimate completion to becoming is made in view of the fact that the process of becoming is never ended by permanent stabilization of a state of being, because everything is in flux. The purpose of the observation is to dispel the illusion of objective realities precisely corresponding to our subjective definitions of things and events. Thus it is said that conventional usages—things as we think and speak of them—are not actually realities corresponding to the way we think and speak of them. This practice is used to foster the ability to understand conceptual descriptions and not be unconsciously mesmerized by them into erroneous attitudes and beliefs.

78.

"Nonbeing" expresses unreality, or untruth. And in nonbeing there is neither cultivation nor deconstruction. It is on account of unreality that beings cultivate and deconstruct; there is nothing that can be brought into existence.

Why? All things have nonexistent intrinsic being; they are void of being, in terms of substance or essence. There is nothing therein that can be cultivated or brought into existence.

When a bodhisattva is practicing perfect insight viewing things this way, one neither cultivates nor deconstructs anything. This is called cultivation of perfect insight.

Practicing thus, abiding thus, one reaches complete fulfillment of the perfect insight of a bodhisattva-mahasattva.

No thought featuring fixation on form occurs to a bodhisattva-mahasattva practicing perfect insight; nor does any thought featuring fixation on sensation, cognition, conditionings, or consciousness. No thought with harsh rigidity occurs. No thought with intolerance occurs. No thought with jealousy occurs. No thought with affliction occurs. No thought with laziness occurs. No thought with distraction occurs. No thought with stupidity occurs. No thought with desire occurs. No thought with fixation on objectification of form occurs. No thought with yearning occurs. No thought with divisiveness occurs. No thought with false views occurs. No thought with obsession with enjoyment occurs. No thought with attachment to power or authority occurs. No thought with attachment to birth in a great family occurs. No thought with attachment to divine rebirth occurs. No thought with attachment to the realm of desire occurs. No thought with attachment to the realms of form and formlessness occurs. No thought about the stage of listeners occurs. No thought about the stage of individual illuminates occurs. No thought with obsession or attachment toward bodhisattva practice occurs. Not even any thought with a notion of nirvana occurs.

COMMENTARY

Zen master Guishan (Kuei-shan) said, "Sages since time immemorial have only explained the problems of pollution. If one does not have all that false consciousness, emotional and intellectual opinionatedness, and conceptual habituation, then one is clear as autumn water, pure and uncontrived, placid and uninhibited. Such people are called wayfarers, or free people." (*The Five Houses of Zen*)

79.

One with this purity of thought pervades beings with goodwill, compassion, joyfulness, and equanimity; and the concept of a being is thereby deconstructed, and one does not stand on the concept of a being or become obsessed while practicing these four states of spiritual expansion, and insight becomes endowed with skill in means. One endowed with these qualities who practices perfect insight will quickly arrive at fulfillment of cultivation of perfect insight.

COMMENTARY

The methodical use of negation in perfect insight scriptures (and Zen literature too) has been subject to negative or nihilistic misinterpretations throughout its history. This is explicitly noted in scriptures themselves (see, for example, the chapter on "essencelessness" in the *Sandhinirmocana-sutra* translated in *Buddhist Yoga*) and is very prominent in the writings and records of the Huayan and Zen schools. This particular passage of the *Questions of Suvikrantavikramin* sutra on perfect insight, on the conscious "pervasion of all beings" with goodwill, compassion, joyfulness, and equanimity, is undoubtedly among the most eloquent illustrations of the truth that the *via negativa* of perfect insight methodology does not end in any sort of moral, mental, or social negativity.

The deconstruction of the "being" by means of the states of spiritual expansion means that the boundaries of the ego are penetrated and one senses the being of all beings as one great body, suffused with goodwill, compassion, joy, and equanimity. It is penetrating insight that enables one to "pervade" all beings without boundaries of "self." In the process of using the penetrating clarity of insight to pervade all beings with goodwill, compassion, joy, and equanimity, skill in means—that is means of helping others to liberation and enlightenment—are developed by way of empathic intimacy with the conditions of all states of being.

80.

The one cultivating perfect insight does not arrive at form or grasp it; nor does one arrive at or grasp sensation, cognition, conditionings, or consciousness. One does not arrive at or grasp unreality, nirvana, or the contents of views. One does not arrive at or grasp the realm of desire, the realm of form, or the realm of formlessness; annihilation or eternity; interdependent occurrence; the elements of earth, water, fire, and air; greed, hatred, or folly; generosity, stinginess, morality, or immorality; tolerance, hostility, diligence, laziness, meditation, distraction, wisdom, or stupidity; points of mindfulness, correct efforts, annulment of errors, immeasurables, or bases of spiritual powers; faculties, powers, branches of enlightenment, meditation, liberation, attainment, superknowledge; suffering, its origination, its extinction, or the path to its extinction; knowledge of nonorigination, knowledge of ending, or knowledge of nonconstruction; the realm of self, the realm of beings, or the realm of phenomena; the stage of ordinary people, the stage of hearers, the stage of individual illuminates, or complete perfect buddhahood; principles and states of ordinary people, hearers, or individual illuminates; knowledge and vision of past, future, and present; unattached knowledge and vision; knowledge, powers, and confidences of buddhas; or interferences or obstacles.

Why? Because all things are unattained, not arrived at, ungrasped, not attained by anyone. For no thing is graspable, nor is anything grasped by anyone. Why? There is nothing therein to grasp or be grasped. Why? All things are pithless, being like illusions. All things are dependent, their essence not to be

found. All things are like re
able. All things are void, in
existent. All things are like
being burst. All things are
and disappear. All things ar
apprehension. All things a
being pithless. All things ar
being ungraspable. All thin;
being based on mere conce;
ent, in that they do not in
gripless, having no intrinsic

Observing all things thu
arrive at anything, or grasp anything, or master anything, or
make a practice of devotion or attachment to anything.

This is a bodhisattva's practice of perfect insight by nonbe-
lief in all things, by nonpossessiveness, by nonattachment, by
nonobsession. The cultivation of perfect insight by a bodhisattva practicing thus reaches fulfillment.

COMMENTARY

Ungraspability is realized as a firsthand experience by trying to grasp
the essence of things mentally. Observing things as ungraspable and
having nothing to grip or gain, nothing to believe or hold, is not done
by thinking about a notion of ungraspability but by bringing phenomena to mind and mentally scrutinizing them for irreducible realities. In
this way ungraspability is not simply taken in as a notion but discovered firsthand as a fact of life at the deepest levels of experiential
reality.

Furthermore, a bodhisattva learning this way does not learn about
form, does not learn about transcendence of form; one does not learn
about sensation, cognition, conditionings, or consciousness; one does
not learn about transcendence of consciousness. One does not learn
about the occurrence of form, one does not learn about the cessation
of form; similarly, one does not learn about the occurrence or cessa-

nition, conditionings, or consciousness. One
ine of form, or unruliness; similarly, one does not
nondiscipline of sensation, cognition, condition-
ousness. One does not learn the transmission of form or
on of form; one does not learn continuity or discontinuity.
me way one does not learn the passage, conception, continu-
discontinuity of sensation, cognition, conditionings, or con-
ousness.

A bodhisattva learning in this way does not learn permanence of
form, does not learn pleasurability of form, does not learn painfulness
of form, does not learn purity of form, does not learn selflessness of
form; one does not learn permanence of sensation, cognition, conditionings, or consciousness; one does not learn painfulness of consciousness, purity of consciousness, or selflessness of consciousness.

COMMENTARY

At this stage of understanding, all of these views have already been
scrutinized and penetrated.

81.

A bodhisattva learning thus does not deal with objectification
of the past of form, does not deal with objectification of the
future of form, does not deal with objectification of the present
of form; one does not deal with objectification of the past of
sensation, cognition, conditionings, or consciousness, does not
deal with objectification of the future and does not deal with
objectification of the present.

COMMENTARY

One of the limitations of our effectiveness is our limited access to past
and future. Memory and foresight are limited not only quantitatively
by preoccupations and preconceptions but also qualitatively. There
may be potentially valuable information in past experience that we do

not use because our memory acts selectively on an emotional basis unsuitable to identifying subtler elements of experience. There may also be essential perceptions of the future consequences of our present acts that we do not see because we are too engrossed in the subjective sensations associated with what we are doing. If we objectify past, future, and present, failing to recognize continuity, our mental relationship to events will not be flexible and free enough to act objectively in a genuine manner, no matter how sincere and intelligent we would like to think we are.

82.

A bodhisattva practicing thus views the past as void, as ceased, as selfless, without even thinking that what is past is void, thus ceased and selfless.

One views the future as empty, null, and selfless, without even thinking that what is yet to come is empty, null, and selfless.

One views the present as empty, null, and selfless, without even thinking that what is present is empty, null, and selfless.

The past is empty and null; one does not even consider it as selfless, as not pertaining to self, impermanent, insubstantial, inconstant, or changing.

The future is empty and null; one does not even consider it as selfless, as not pertaining to self, impermanent, insubstantial, inconstant, or changing.

The present is empty and null; one does not even consider it as selfless, not pertaining to self, impermanent, insubstantial, inconstant, or changing.

COMMENTARY

Zen master Muso said, "Essentially it may be said that there are two kinds of aspiration for enlightenment, the shallow and the true. Understanding that whatever is born must die, that whatever flourishes must decline, forgetting worldly ambitions and only seeking the way to emancipation—this is called the shallow aspiration for enlightenment." *(Dream Conversations)* Dealing as it does with "graduate" studies, the perfect insight teaching presupposes that the practitioner has already passed through this stage of "shallow aspiration for enlightenment" and subsequently penetrates intuitively without linear process.

83.

Furthermore, a bodhisattva practicing thus does not cling to form or sensation or cognition or conditionings or consciousness. One does not cling to name and form, one does not cling to error and opinion, one does not cling to a false idea of self, one does not cling to a false idea of a being, one does not cling to annihilation or permanence, one does not cling to the finite or the infinite. One does not cling to form or color, sound, scent, flavor, texture, or phenomenon; the realms of desire, form, and formlessness; interdependent occurrence; the elements of earth, water, fire, air, and space; truth or falsehood; attachment or detachment; greed, hatred, or folly; abandonment of greed, hatred, and folly; generosity, stinginess, morality, or immorality; tolerance or hostility; diligence or laziness; meditation or distraction; wisdom or stupidity; points of mindfulness, right efforts, bases of spiritual powers, or annulments of error; faculties, powers, or branches of enlightenment; concentrations or attainments; goodwill, compassion, joy, equanimity; knowledge of nonorigination, knowledge of ending, or knowledge of noncreation; stages of ordinary people, hearers, or individual illuminates; practices of ordinary people, hearers, or individual illuminates; suffering, its origin, its extinction, or the path to extinction; superknowledge or knowledge and vision; liberation, or knowledge and vision of liberation; nirvana; knowledge and vision of past, future, and present; knowledge without attachments; buddha knowledge; powers and confidences of buddhas; purification of buddha lands; purification of external appearances; accomplishments of hearers, individual illuminates, or bodhisattvas.

Why? Because all things are groundless. For there is noth-ing in anything to grasp, wherein would be its ground.

As long as there is clinging, there is trying, there is grasp-ing. As long as there is grasping, as long as there is clinging, so long is there discomfort and distress, so long are there sure to be sorrow, pain, unease, and lament.

COMMENTARY

Persons without autonomy who are engrossed in intellectual, psycho-logical, and behavioral habits that hinder and harm may be induced to engross themselves in more wholesome habits in order to improve them. The practice of perfect insight comes after this stage of human development and does not cling obsessively to anything, even the good and the wholesome. An example of the relative positions of these two stages of development was given earlier, where scripture says that the first five perfections—charity, morality, tolerance, diligence, and meditation—soften the heart to prepare it for perfect insight.

The present passage also explains an earlier scriptural statement that it is nonetheless the perfection of insight that perfects the other prac-tices, and the perfection of insight that penetrates to liberation. With-out insight, religious or spiritual practices are still infected with clinging, trying, and grasping, and under those conditions they thereby produce discomfort and distress, sorrow and lament. This can be witnessed and verified in actuality by any who care to investigate the matter from this perspective.

84.

To the extent that there is clinging, to that extent is there bondage. To the extent that there is clinging, to that extent is there no path—to that extent all is discomfort and distress. As long as there is clinging, so long is there vain imagination, projection, and conceptual complication.

As long as there is clinging, there is contention, dissent, and argumentation.

As long as there is clinging, there is ignorance, darkness, and folly.

As long as there is clinging, there are fears, there are horrors.

As long as there is clinging, there is the snare of morbidity and the destructiveness of morbidity.

As long as there is clinging, there is harassment by discomfort and seeking of comfort.

The bodhisattva seeing these and all the rest does not cling to anything at all. Not clinging, one does not grasp anything at all, and does not make a practice of taking up or holding to everything, and does not even think of anything as groundless and nonindependent.

COMMENTARY

A Zen proverb says, "Even though gold dust is precious, when stuck in the eyes it obstructs vision."

Afterword

WARNINGS ON THE LABEL

As a teacher, Buddha is traditionally likened to a physician, who pre-
scribes specific medicines according to the particular ailments. That is
why it is said, even in scriptures, that there is no fixed teaching.

Just as ordinary medicines have their indications and contraindications—what they are good for and when they should be avoided—so
do the spiritual "medicines" of Buddhism. Zen master Baizhang said,
"If you don't have the disease, don't take the medicine."

There is not only the matter of whether or not a remedy suits an
ailment but also the question of whether or not the afflicted constitution is able to respond positively to the remedy. A system radically
weakened by illness may not be able to withstand intensive treatment.
Zen master Baizhang said, "The universal teaching of Buddhism is like
elixir, but it is also like poison. If you can digest it, it is like elixir; if
you cannot digest it, it is like poison."

There is an extensive list of contraindications for the teachings on
perfection of insight in the *Suvikrantavikrami-pariprccha Prajnaparamita-
sutra*. While they are in the beginning of the original document, in
translation they are more easily understood for what they are from the
perspective of the expositions of insight and emptiness in the body of
the book. The most elementary degree of insight makes it clear why

certain mentalities effectively exclude themselves from the experience and how it would adversely affect them to taste emptiness.

This is not, of course, an absolute exclusion, for none of these states is permanent in nature and under certain conditions they can be changed for the better. The various teachings presented for that purpose are also mentioned in the literature on insight, in reference to the courses of cultivation from which the practitioners of insight have graduated. This gives the unripe a way to approach the insight teachings in a gradual manner and also buffers and balances the insight teachings themselves.

In this sense, the list of contraindications—people with mentalities for which the teachings are not recommended—also provides a framework for preliminary self-examination, through which one may approach insight by way of psychological housecleaning. The following are those who scripture indicates cannot in their present state benefit from the insight teachings.

People with low aspirations, in the context of Mahayana Buddhism, this usually refers to people who covet personal peace for its own sake, as an object of desire. This mind-set typically interprets the teachings on emptiness in terms of escapism, nihilism, and oblivion.

People with a pauper's mentality, meaning a mind plagued with ever present hankering and insecurity. In this condition the mind is always subconsciously trying to get hold of something solid, always trying to rest on something, always trying to "set up housekeeping," so the "nongrasping" procedures of insight practice cause great anxiety and cannot be tolerated.

The pauper's mentality can also mean the tendency to think too much of too little. In this context it refers to subconscious haste to take a shallow interpretation of the teachings for their full import. The "belly" is swelled up for a time by this intake, but there is no real nutrition, only a suggestion of fullness.

Lazy people, and people overcome by indolence and sloth, are excluded as well. This character habit also tends to bias the mind toward superficiality. In this context, superficiality in reception of the teachings on emptiness may mean literalism and/or nihilist escapism, both of which are forms of studied irrelevance.

People sunk in the mire of views cannot see through the external formulations of the teachings to arrive at their own import, because everything they consider is made into a view. In any case, those who are completely immersed in their own worldviews ordinarily do not have any interest in a teaching that tells them their views are not really true and their world is not truly real. For those sunk in views, everything is construed to reflect their views in some way, even by seeming opposition. There is no way to transcendence within this loop, by dint of the very fact that it is enclosed by wraparound subjective views.

People bound by the noose of temptation, whose subconscious minds are constantly nagging them with impulses, fancies, and whims. If people in this condition use the deconstruction techniques of the insight teachings to relax their reason, instead of attaining liberation they may unconsciously abandon themselves to inner whisperings and imagine they are free.

Shameless people, who construe teachings on emptiness in a pseudointellectual way to rationalize license of all sorts and may also concentrate on objectification of emptiness as some variety of "nothingness" to achieve oblivion in order to enable themselves to ignore most of the consequences of their actions.

Also listed are numerous other characteristics analogous or related to shamelessness that similarly predispose people to react to insight and emptiness teachings in unhealthy ways, or that make these teachings inaccessible or harmful to them. Like the shameless, the insatiable, those mired in lust and desires, the importunate, the ungrateful, the immoral, and those inclined to evil are all prone to unconsciously appropriate the teachings for moral and mental license.

Absent-minded, scatterbrained, and unseeing people are also unable to benefit from the teachings on perfect insight because they lack the focus, concentration, and perceptivity to withstand the dissolution of conventional constructs and conventions and still maintain psychological integrity.

Deceivers, tricksters, charlatans, talkers, fortune-tellers, and their ilk are all apt to employ teachings on emptiness to convince their marks that since conventional conceptions and usages are all "empty" and ultimately untrue, then anything incomprehensible or irrational might be true. This form of abuse may seem quite primitive, but it is still active around the globe, including in the West, where scientific debunking of traditional ideas has not by any means eradicated old superstitions.

On the contrary, scientific "discovery" of nonabsoluteness in many areas where we are accustomed to take our conventional sense of reality for granted has been used in some domains of Western culture to create a climate in which illusions about less familiar realities, such as spirituality, can be sheltered from critical analysis. The crux of this disorder is confusion about the meanings of negation in Buddhist teaching, which can be used to deceive oneself, even unconsciously, and to deceive and defraud others, whether consciously or unconsciously, whether deliberately or compulsively. As the seventeenth-century Zen master Bunan remarked, "People hear there is no good or bad and think that means bad is good."

Gone, gone, gone beyond, gone beyond the beyond.

Text Sources

Scripture on Perfect Insight Awakening to Essence, translated into Chinese by Weijing of the Song dynasty (960–1279). Either a retranslation of the original or a reworking of an older translation, this text contains some useful nonstandard terminology and adroitly connects the Prajnapara-mita and Yogachara teachings of Buddhism.

Essentials of the Great Scripture on Perfect Insight is a treatise by the great seventh-century Korean Buddhist author Won Hyol. According to a traditional story, Won Hyol intended to go to China, then flourishing culturally under the early Tang dynasty, in order to study Buddhism. One night in a mountain cave on the way to China, Won Hyol rose in the night feeling very thirsty. Groping in the dark, he happened to find a bowl with some liquid in it. Since pilgrims often used mountain caves, he saw nothing strange about this. Drinking the liquid from the bowl, he found it sweet and refreshing. Having quenched his thirst, he went back to sleep. When he woke the next morning, however, in the light of day Won Hyol saw that he had drunk putrid matter from a human skull. Horrified and revolted, Won Hyol vomited. Then he reflected that he had in fact tasted the liquid as sweet the night before when he thought he was drinking from a bowl. That experience taught him the truth of vijnaptimatrata, or "representation only," and he thereupon became enlightened. With no more need to study Buddhism, Won Hyol turned around and went back to Korea.

Treatise on the Great Scripture on Perfect Insight, attributed to the great Indian master Nagarjuna (traditionally ca. first century BCE–first century CE), who is famous for his works on the subject of shunyata, or emptiness. Nagarjuna is sometimes called the second Buddha, such was his great contribution to the understanding of Buddha's teachings. Nagarjuna is considered an ancestor of all the major schools of Buddhism, including Zen, Tantra, and Pure Land Buddhism. Legend attributes to Nagarjuna the recovery of the entire body of the Prajnaparamita Sutras on perfect insight from storage in the realm of the Nagas, whose name means "dragon." These were an indigenous people of India whose culture was not well known to Brahmin orthodoxy; Nagas are said to have attended the discourses of Buddha, and they may indeed have preserved certain teachings disregarded by the ex-Brahmins of the Buddhist sangha. It has also been said that the meaning of the "dragon" association is actually the psychic force sometimes known as *kundalini,* used by Nagarjuna and the Tantrics to gain access to nondiscursive knowledge by temporarily effacing ratiocination. Nagarjuna's name means "dragon tree," and this has been used to suggest the imagery of kundalini psychic force rising up the spine and into the head. Both Buddha and Nagarjuna are also portrayed as being sheltered by a great snake rising up behind them and over their heads; this has been taken to symbolize kundalini.

Many texts have been attributed to Nagarjuna that may or may not be the work of one man. This famous treatise/commentary on the great scripture on perfect insight, often known by its Chinese name *Dazhidulun (Ta-chih-tu Lun),* is traditionally ascribed to Nagarjuna, but there is some controversy over this. Some say that the great translator Kumarajiva (ca. 400 CE), who is credited with rendering this massive text into Chinese, was actually the author. Certainly there are materials from many sources in this treatise, ranging from dictionary- and encyclopedia-type sources to folkloric and literary sources.

Scripture on Perfect Insight for Benevolent Rulers, officially recorded as having been translated into Chinese by the great Kumarajiva, may have been composed by him, or may have been a Central Asian sutra com-

piled during what Chinese historians call the era of the Sixteen Kingdoms, when numerous Central Asian kingdoms intimately connected
with China rose and fell. These kingdoms were established by tribes
who incorporated elements of Indo-Buddhist and Chinese cultures
into their own, producing new hybrid Buddhist civilizations in Central
Asia. Kumarajiva was actually kidnapped and taken captive on the or-
ders of one of those kings, who made Kumarajiva live in his capital to
translate Buddhist texts and teach Buddhism for the development of
the kingdom's new culture. Kumarajiva was a renowned genius, and
the king who had him captured provided him with ten wives in order
to reproduce more geniuses for the good of the culture. These circumstances may shed some light on Kumarajiva's motivations for producing this scripture, or a scripture like this, which may nevertheless have
been his own compilation or presentation of scriptural teachings rather
than his own composition per se.

Key Teachings of the Great Scripture on Perfect Insight is a systematic reduction of Xuanzang's gigantic six-hundred-scroll Chinese translation
of the scripture, made by Dayin of the Song dynasty. The reduction
process is based on abbreviation of formulaic repetitions to focus on
the key principles of the teaching. This work is very convenient for
gaining an overview of what is otherwise an extraordinarily immense
scripture, even for Mahayana Buddhism. This distillation of the keys
of the scripture remained little known until it was "discovered" in the
memory of an otherwise unidentified "strange monk" (or "foreign
monk") and published by a group of lay Buddhists in the late twelfth
century. It was later reprinted in the middle of the fourteenth century.

The Questions of Suvikrantavikramin is one of the Prajnaparamita Sutras,
scriptures on perfect insight, that still exist in Sanskrit. The Sanskrit
used is generally fairly classical but includes some Buddhist readings
and plays on words that cannot be mechanically resolved by standard
classical protocols. This is one of the beauties of this text in that it
illustrates a useful feature of the broad spectrum of so-called Buddhist
Hybrid Sanskrit, namely the nonexistence of a standardized grammati-
cal or semantic protocol, which allows for adaptation of technical terminology from the Sanskrit language to different cultural, textual, and
metaphysical contexts.

The selections of Suvikranta's questions, one of the subtlest of the sutras, are presented here translated from the original Sanskrit, for which I have used Ryusho Hikata's 1958 edition of *Suvikrantavikrami-pariprccha Prajnaparamita-sutra*, published by Rinsen Book Company, Kyoto, 1983.

Commentary Sources

The Blue Cliff Record. Translated by Thomas Cleary and J. C. Cleary. Boston: Shambhala Publications, 1977. This is one of the most valued of koan collections, with several layers of commentary on Zen stories by great Zen masters.

Buddhist Yoga: A Comprehensive Course. Translated by Thomas Cleary. Boston: Shambhala Publications, 1995. This is a translation of the *Sandhinirmocana-sutra,* one of the main scriptural sources for Yogachara Buddhism. The second, third, fourth, and fifth chapters are particularly relevant to understanding the teaching of perfect insight.

Dream Conversations on Buddhism and Zen. Zen master Muso Soseki, translated by Thomas Cleary. Boston: Shambhala Publications, 1994. This book presents an English version of one of the rare Zen classics of Japanese origin, based on the conversations of Zen master Muso Soseki (1275–1351), who was a Zen mentor of two shoguns and was also named Kokushi, or Teacher of the Nation, by seven emperors. Muso was brought up in the esoteric Tantric tradition before studying Zen with Chinese and Japanese masters and was also known to use the *Source Mirror Record,* a massive compilation of extracts from scriptures and treatises with expositions, disseminating Zen in harmony with the classical teachings of Buddhism. This book deals with basic issues of psychological, religious, and spiritual strivings from a Zen Buddhist point of view and is especially useful for the general reader.

The Essential Confucius. Translated and presented by Thomas Cleary. San Francisco: HarperCollins, 1992. These sayings of Confucius, some of which have been related to Buddhist teachings in annotations, are examples of the sort of common-sense material that people would normally have already imbibed before concentrating on penetrating world-transcending insight.

The Five Houses of Zen. Thomas Cleary. Boston: Shambhala Publications, 1997. This is an anthology of teachings from the classical age of Zen in China.

The Flower Ornament Scripture: A Translation of the Avatamsaka Sutra. Translated by Thomas Cleary. Boston: Shambhala, 1984, 1986, 1987, 1989, 1993. This scripture is the most comprehensive of all Buddhist sutras in terms of the spectrum of teachings it contains. Within the scripture, books nine through fourteen and book sixteen contain special focus on emptiness and the perfect insight teaching.

Instant Zen: Waking Up in the Present. Translated by Thomas Cleary. Berkeley: North Atlantic Books, 1994. This is a collection of translations from the speeches of the outstanding twelfth-century Zen master Foyan. This master's teaching is unusually subtle and contains a great many do-it-yourself insight exercises.

Kensho: The Heart of Zen. Thomas Cleary. Boston: Shambhala Publications, 1997. This is a set of Zen teachings from Korea, Japan, and China focusing on the awakening of intuitive insight and its operation in the aftermath of awakening.

The teachings from China are selected from one of the major collections of koans, or Zen stories, showing how these stories are used to foster insight effectively.

The teachings from Japan are rare writings of the famous Zen master Hakuin (1686–1769), an outstanding reviver of Rinzai Zen who is popularly considered the greatest Japanese Zen saint of the last five hundred years. These writings deal with various subjects, but in each case Hakuin interprets classical scriptural and Zen themes from the point of view of activating intuitive insight.

The teachings from Korea consist of a famous treatise on mind by the great master Chinul (1158–1210), integrating Zen and scriptural teachings focusing on insight and its application.

Shobogenzo: Zen Essays by Dogen. Translated by Thomas Cleary. Honolulu: University Press of Hawaii, 1986. This is a set of annotated translations of thirteen original essays by the bold and brilliant thirteenth-century Zen master Dogen (1200–1253). Dogen was originally a monk of the Tendai order, many of whose main meditation methods are based on the emptiness and perfect insight teachings, including the writings of Nagarjuna. Later Dogen became a Rinzai Zen master, then a Soto Zen master. His various speeches and writings reflect Dogen's mastery of all of these schools. This particular collection contains a great deal of Zen material, but it is used to illustrate the contemplative practices of all the schools of Buddhism, including Tendai, Shingon, and Zen, which are interwoven in Dogen's work.

Stopping and Seeing: A Comprehensive Course in Buddhist Meditation. Chih-i, translated by Thomas Cleary. Boston: Shambhala Publications, 1997. This is from the classic *Mohe Zhiguan,* an extensive and detailed treatise on meditation by the founder of Tiantai Buddhism. Many of the methods of contemplation expounded in this text are based on Nagarjuna's work on emptiness.

The Sutra of Hui-neng, Grand Master of Zen. Translated by Thomas Cleary. Boston: Shambhala Publications, 1998. This is a collection of speeches attributed to the most popular of the early Zen founders. The second lecture is all about prajna, or insight. Included is a translation of a commentary attributed to the master on the *Diamond Sutra,* one of the best known of the scriptures on perfect insight.

Zen Essence: The Science of Freedom. Translated and edited by Thomas Cleary. Boston: Shambhala Publications, 1989. This is a collection of extracts from the sayings of great Chinese Zen masters from the Tang to the Yuan dynasties, focusing particularly on practical methods of exercising intuitive insight.